Dear Aris,

Thank you for your excellent work ethic and support this last few weeks. Looking forward to working alongside you clinically now as a fellow associate!

Thank you!

Ben

THE
NATURAL
GARDENER

JOHN HARRIS
WITH JIM RICKARDS

THE
NATURAL
GARDENER

A Lifetime of Gardening
of the Phases of
the Moon

metro

First published in the UK by John Blake Publishing
an imprint of Bonnier Books UK
80-81 Wimpole Street, London, W1G 9RE

Owned by Bonnier Books
Sveavägen 56, Stockholm, Sweden

www.facebook.com/johnblakebooks
twitter.com/jblakebooks

First published in hardback in 2016, this edition published in 2020

Hardback ISBN: 978-1-78946-280-7
Ebook ISBN: 978-1-78606-318-2

All rights reserved. No part of this publication may be reproduced, stored in a retrieval system, or transmitted in any form or by any means, without the prior permission in writing of the publisher, nor be otherwise circulated in any form of binding or cover other than that in which it is published and without a similar condition including this condition being imposed on the subsequent purchaser.

British Library Cataloguing-in-Publication Data:
A catalogue record for this book is available from the British Library.

Design by www.envydesign.co.uk

Printed and bound in Great Britain by Clays Ltd, Elcograf S.p.A.

1 3 5 7 9 10 8 6 4 2

Text copyright © John Harris and Jim Rickards 2016
Internal illustrations copyright © Claire Buchan 2016
Cover Illustration copyright © by James Weston Lewis 2020

The right of John Harris and Jim Rickards to be identified as the authors of this work has been asserted by them in accordance with the Copyright, Designs and Patents Act 1988.

Every reasonable effort has been made to trace copyright-holders of material reproduced in this book, but if any have been inadvertently overlooked the publishers would be glad to hear from them.

Metro Publishing is an imprint of Bonnier Books UK
www.bonnierbooks.co.uk

Contents

Introduction: New Moon
Armed with a hoe and an open mind . . . 1

PART ONE: My Lunatic Life and Learnings: A potted history from beginnings to now 3
1. There's Methodist to my Madness 5
2. Spades and Alchemy 15
3. Meet the Head Gardener 25
4. Moons and New Orbits 31
5. Rex the Rogue 37
6. 'The Clearance' 43
7. Tresillian Today 51

PART TWO: Harnessing the Power of the Moon in Your Garden: How to grow more and better for less effort and cost   57

  8. The Rise, Fall and Rise of Growing Your Own   59
  9. It's All About the Soil   63
 10. The Four Quarters of the Moon: Overview and General Principles   65
 11. The Four Quarters in Detail   77
 12. Making Time for the Moon   91
 13. Superpowering Moon Gardening   93
 14. Crop Rotation   97
 15. Make Your Bed and Grow In It   107
 16. pH – The Power of Hydrogen   125
 17. Friends and Enemies – the Secrets of Compatible Planting   133
 18. Fertilisers, Manures and Feeds   139
 19. Stand Your Ground   165

PART THREE: The Proof is in the Planting . . . and the pruning, and the trading, and the fishing   167

 20. When We Stopped Moving, We Started Growing   169
 21. How the Moon Helped Those Before Us   173
 22. Studies of the Moon's Effect on Plants   187

| 23. Studies of the Moon's Effect on Animals (Including Us) | 193 |
| 24. Last Thoughts | 199 |

PART FOUR: Appendixes
Grow What You Know, Know What You Grow: Develop deep-rooted knowledge, watch your garden flourish, share what you learn — 205

Appendix I: Useful Resources	207
Appendix II: Further Reading	219
Appendix III: Frequently Asked Questions	223

Coda: New Moon — 231

My 2020–2022 Moon Gardening Calendars — 233
Acknowledgements — 237

DEDICATION

I would like to dedicate this book to the three men who influenced my life:

My father, whom I knew but for a short time

Uncle Jack (Honey) – when I needed a father figure, he was there

And Noel Masters, who set me on the path to where I have arrived today

Preface to the Second Edition

How it all began...

I have always found solace in the soil. Even in some very tough times, gardening has provided for me. As is explained later, the events of my childhood led to an early introduction to life on the allotment and the sheer joy which one experiences when growing your own. I owe so much to those men on the allotments, I was lucky that some of them tucked me under their wing and channelled my energy into learning how to do things well from the start before trying to take on the whole world.

They were hard task masters at times but they taught me there were no shortcuts, there was only the right way. Most of them had been in the Second World War, some had survived both. They carried scars with them, but they always had time to teach me not only gardening, but life skills such as hard work and always making time for a troubled person along the way.

It grounded me at a time when I could have gone very

wayward. And it gave me the passion and the knowledge to build a career in horticulture that has shaped my life for the better. (Starting at the age of fifteen working on a private estate for the princely sum of £1,19 shillings and a single penny for a forty-eight-hour week.)

To this day, I've always been a professional horticulturist. But, unlike many, I grow vegetables, fruit and flowers with the help of three of the industry's oldest and least-used tools: the moon, understanding plants' ability to help each other to thrive or to perish, and knowledge of how gardeners worked before the arrival of today's technology.

I'm grateful to those old men on the allotment. What I learned under their guidance gave me a flourishing career, culminating in the chance to take the reins at the wonderful Tresillian Estate. I was given full responsibility and a free hand to restore their derelict Victorian walled kitchen garden. It was my one big chance to put into practice all I had learned. To prove how the influence of the lunar cycle, compatible planting, and organic feeding and management can increase yields and food quality for lower cost and ultimately lower effort.

Standing in the shoes and occupying the minds of those head gardeners before me, I pursued a programme of research into yesterday's plants and yesterday's methods. Along the way, I've sourced and preserved many heritage varieties of crops, some dating back centuries, that were on the verge of disappearing altogether. I ran the kitchen garden entirely organically, using traditional techniques that were barely remembered. The results were spectacular. Bigger, tastier, juicer fruit and veg for the table, produced more economically and with no chemicals.

PREFACE TO THE SECOND EDITION

This brought about much interest from the gardening world, including appearances on the BBC's *Garden Stories*.

With well over sixty years in gardening and seeing a lifetime of changes where you can get out-of-season strawberries on Christmas Day and first-class plants delivered through your letterbox, I accept and am happy that we are living in an ever-changing world as far as gardening is concerned. But I also truly believe that good practice is best achieved by accumulating knowledge, not replacing it.

The Romans, the Greeks, the Romanies, the Native Americans, the Māoris, in fact most ancient civilizations, used the moon as their gardening calendar, and natural friends and enemies in the plant world, to get the most from their crops. I'm not anti-technology, just pro-preservation. Sometimes practices that work simply and efficiently are lost in the name of 'progress'.

I hope I still have a fair few deep trenches left in me. But before I myself become compost, I want to pass on as much of what I have learned as possible, just as those old men on a Newquay allotment did for me all those moons ago.

John Harris
July 2020

…And How to Keep it Going

This book was originally published in 2016 under the title: *Moon Gardening: Learn Ancient and Natural Ways to Grow More and Better with Less*. It was the product of sixty years of John Harris's vast horticultural knowledge and fifteen visits to his home on the Tresillian Estate near Newquay, Cornwall. I sat on his living room sofa, laptop on knee and typed as fast as I could to keep up while he rattled away with enthusiasm and deep respect for his subject.

John is a natural raconteur, full of amazing stories and endless intriguing gardening advice that you're unlikely to hear anywhere else. Because he's a true man of the soil. And a rare breed nowadays – someone who has spent his entire private and commercial life devoted to horticulture. He's also one of the very few people to have been trained as an apprentice by gardeners who in turn earned their spurs in Victorian estate kitchen gardens before most of them died out after the first world war. This means he's seen enormous change in the industry at a professional level. He's watched as the new ways of mass production, out-of-season growing, and widespread use of chemical pesticides and fertilisers have crowded out traditional approaches to gardening in tune with the environment.

We wrote this book to ensure that the unique mix of what John has learned through experience is passed on to others so it isn't lost for ever. Because the ancient ways of gardening to the phases of the moon, using natural feeds and pesticides, and companion planting really do produce incredible results. And they're particularly suitable for the amateur and new gardener alike, whatever the size of their plot. John's belief is that if you're

PREFACE TO THE SECOND EDITION

about to start out on a new venture you might as well learn the best way to do it first time around.

Which brings us to why the book is being re-released now, and under a new title: *The Natural Gardener*. We were keen for new gardeners to know that everything in these pages is accessible and easy to put into practice. In fact, the book is packed with natural tips and tricks that anyone can follow and see great results from.

So whilst underlying all of John's techniques is growing food in accordance with the phases of the moon, the key driving force you'll find on every page is John's passion for passing on invaluable advice that shows you how to manage your garden organically and cheaply. Way before it was popular, John was a strong advocate of recycling in its most fundamental form: 'Anything that comes out of the soil,' he said to me recently, 'can go back into the soil. If it grows, it rots. If it rots, it'll make compost.' All vegetable kitchen waste including cooking water can be recycled and your plants will thrive on it. It's completely natural, and it's free.

This is a theme you'll see cropping up again and again. Where possible, use what you've already got to get your garden going. You don't have to go out and spend a small fortune before you start reaping the rewards of your endeavour. You can get yourself set up at low cost and, by following the advice here, keep running costs to a minimum too – simply by gardening sustainably, and letting nature do most of the hard work for you. For example, next time you boil your spuds, save the cooking water. "It's one of the finest organic sprays for tackling whitefly," says John.

One of the key aims of the first edition of this book was to show new gardeners that with a little planning and the right guidance you can grow abundant crops, cheaply and organically even with a small patch of land. In times of great uncertainty we yearn to feel in control of our lives. The COVID-19 pandemic of 2020 has brought into sharp focus a mood that has been growing steadily over the past decade. We want to know where our food comes from. We care about the effects of the pesticides and chemicals used in mass production – both on ourselves and the world around us. We're worried about the effects of climate change and the contribution that ferrying fruit halfway across the globe may have on it. In short, we feel disconnected from the very thing that keeps us alive.

During the height of the pandemic millions of us were locked in our homes with our own thoughts. Maybe it was the rare time allowed to take stock and reflect, or concern over empty supermarket shelves, or simply the need to keep busy – but many of us turned to our gardens again. It's an activity well-known for relieving anxiety. This was an area we could control and make our own. Consequently, spring 2020 saw a huge boom in amateur gardening. Within a few weeks of the lockdown compost seemed as valuable as gold (or maybe toilet paper).

Suddenly, the renaissance in British food, the celebration of artisan producers, and support for local suppliers chimed with the idea that actually maybe we could go one further and do this ourselves on our own patch? You can't get lower food miles than delivering from your own garden. It feels like going back to 'the old ways', but this isn't just some self-indulgent nostalgia trip. The 'old ways' work. They're healthier, they're kinder to the planet, and they're more economical.

PREFACE TO THE SECOND EDITION

With so many new gardeners now growing their own, we want to encourage them to keep at it, to enjoy the wonder of pulling food straight from your own soil and having it on your plate for tea within minutes. *The Natural Gardener* will show you tried and tested ways to do this organically, encouraging the earth to do what she does so well. As John says: 'We need to tread lightly on the soil, so future generations can do the same.'

Jim Rickards
July 2020

Introduction

New Moon

ARMED WITH A HOE AND AN OPEN MIND . . .

OK, before we start, let's get one thing clarified immediately, because it's the question I get asked more frequently than any other. My approach to Moon Gardening does not mean you have to creep out in the middle of the night, trying desperately not to wake the neighbours, tripping over hoes in the dark with only a miner's lamp and the light of the silvery moon to guide you as you try to work out whether you're pulling up potatoes or parsnips. By all means try it – midnight under a full moon is a magical time to be out, listening for nocturnal life while most human activity is dormant. But I believe the possible positive effect of gardening at this time (and some people do swear by it) is outweighed by the impracticality and sheer hassle for most people. Including me.

So, instead, what if I were to tell you, you could:

- increase your crop yield;
- grow better-tasting food;
- do a bit less work in the garden; and
- save money on fertiliser into the bargain?

You'd probably think I was a lunatic. Well, the truth is, I am. So are you.

We're all lunatics, because pretty much everything on this planet is affected by the moon. Good and bad, minor and major, warm and cold, up and down – the gravitational effects of the moon's orbit around the Earth are apparent in thousands of things we take for granted every day. Not just the tides pulled relentlessly in, out and along the coast, but also the great bodies of water that lie under our feet everywhere: the water table, which rises and falls in tune with the passage of new moon to full moon and back again.

We all know that Earth is influenced by the moon. But so is the earth in your garden, and all the plants that grow from it. *The Natural Gardener* will show you how this knowledge has transformed my horticultural career as head gardener at Cornwall's beautiful Tresillian Estate. It will also explain why it works and how you can put it into practice in your own garden or allotment, no matter the size. All you need is a patch of land, a handful of seed, a fork, a hoe and an open mind.

Part One

My Lunatic Life and Learnings

A potted history from beginnings to now

1

There's Methodist to my Madness

My lifelong fascination with the moon might never have started at all had my father not died when I was so young. I don't remember a great deal about him, but the fragments that remain have shaped much of the way I approach life and the way I think now.

By all accounts Thomas Lewis Harris, known to everybody as Lou, was a kind and thoughtful man. He was a lay preacher, a Methodist to his marrow, well respected by the community, and a bookkeeper for the now defunct Newquay Urban District Council. But these are simple facts, information I've been told at one remove. They fit with my own scant memories, but they don't really give a picture of what type of man he was, moment by moment. The things you see and hear for yourself are what really stay with you.

I was born in Newquay in 1941, and lived with my parents and two sisters in a small terraced house. As in most Cornish towns and villages during that era, everybody knew everybody, and everyone looked out for everyone. It wasn't because we were all especially kind or lived in a particularly nosey community. It was just the way things were done.

My father was a writer of beautiful letters, not just the sentences he created, but the art of the writing itself. He practised calligraphy when he had free time, putting everything to paper in longhand with a dip pen, in intricate, finely wrought and carefully planned copperplate.

Our house had a kitchen in the front, living room in the back. Father had a small desk beside the Cornish range, beside it a rack of pipes of all types: cherrywood, long clay things and ebony mouthpieces. He would place flecks of charcoal, one by one, into the pipe before he tamped in the tobacco from his favourite 'Africando' mix. When he smoked, to the consternation of Mother, it filled the kitchen with a beautiful, sweet, multi-layered smell of manna-from-Heaven food from exotic coastlines – one that I could not equate with the astringent, bitter attack to the tongue I received the one time I nervously took a pipe from the rack and placed it in my mouth. (At fifteen, I was going to be a man and tried again with rolling papers. I nearly choked to death, chucked the pack away and never smoked again.)

In the way memory always simplifies events into neat slots, it seemed that every weekend the sun would stream in through the kitchen window, casting huge shadows on the walls, and Father would sit there in silhouette, bent over his desk, left

My father wrote beautiful letters.

arm flat on the wood, thumb keeping paper in place and right hand slowly working the letters. I used to sit in the kitchen sometimes, just watching him dipping his pens into different-coloured inks, so quietly he would forget I was there. He always concentrated hard, forcing his focus on the task in hand. His desk was a special place for him – I think it felt like a sanctuary from the memories that plagued him from the Great War – and I liked just being there, to share that space with him. It was one of the rare times I could stay still. As a young child, I was forever needing to 'do' things – whether that was building dams in the brook nearby or climbing trees in the orchard, running errands for Mother or spearing flatfish with a bamboo and nail in the River Gannell.

But in the kitchen with Father I could just *be*. There was an absorbing calmness in watching him work. The only things that ever distracted me in that room were the motes dancing in the sunlight. I often wondered if they'd ever settle on the ground.

Sometimes, Father would not look up from his letters for an hour or more. When he did, it would be to uncurl his spine and crick his neck back into place, then he'd lean back over until the job was finished. That was the level of care he put into what for him was both a passion and a duty. For it was due to his mastery of a craft that he was asked to write numerous letters within our community: official letters, personal letters, letters of condolence and of reference. The end product was always a thing of assured beauty, always fitting to the subject matter, and it taught me, even at that young age, that enthusiasm coupled with serious engagement to something could create great things. It's an easy, pat phrase: 'If a thing's worth doing, it's worth doing well.' But, if you live by this, you get your rewards – and so do the people around you.

For as long as I remember, Father suffered from ill health. It could have been shrapnel or shellshock, I never found out. All I know is it took its toll on him. Which may explain why he was a man of contradictions (maybe we all are): as a lay preacher he was a strict disciplinarian, yet would go out of his way to be kind and offer warm thoughts; he also seemed to be a reserved, removed man, yet he was known by everyone. In the end he was simply my father and I loved him unquestioningly as any young son would.

When he wasn't bent over his letters, he'd sit quietly in his chair by our Cornish range and read the Bible. Sometimes he'd quote from it to raise a point and he'd expect us to listen and take heed. He was a Methodist minister, after all; it was what he did. I can't say my attention didn't wander when the mini-sermons began to build – I was just a child, whose thoughts buzzed everywhere, and I fear God was not always the guider of their direction. But I knew my father was very straight, dependable and honest, and I looked up to him.

Although, after the war, people did have a strong sense of community, and although Father was widely respected in Newquay, it still, in the end, didn't bring the money in or guarantee food on the table. In the late forties, the world was a harsh place for the weak. We'd defeated Nazism, but, for many working-class and rural families, that was simply the first battle won. The war of 'making ends meet' drew us into everyday skirmishes with the taxman, the tallyman and the savings pot under the mattress, and it seemed to offer no prospect of a final and decisive victory. So my mum had to go out all hours to take on menial jobs. She juggled keeping house with helping out in the kitchen of a stray auntie's café down the road. In the evening she'd bring out a great heap of clothes from neighbours and start darning, determined to fix our world stitch by stitch. Which meant my two sisters, Mena and Hilda, and I needed looking after or we'd be running wild.

Now, we wouldn't have minded that – though we had little in material wealth, there was an enormous freedom that I think is lost to the modern child. We had dangerous, exciting worlds to explore and, once out of sight of adults, few rules to abide by or fears to check us. Unfortunately, nowadays, with the great privilege of mass communication and endless knowledge comes the sad balance that children are forced to grow up too early, instilled with worries by parents who understandably care for them and love them almost too much.

Though my sisters were more stay-at-home than I was, I'd tempt them out every now and then. We'd spend all day picking blackberries and come home with our faces purple. And, if they were too nervous to join me, I'd team up with my friends and we'd nick apples from the local orchards (orchards I'd later help revive beyond all recognition). We didn't think we'd had a proper day out unless we'd been chased by angry farmers over hedgerows. We loved it. Getting dirty, being naughty and wondering only what adventure the next day would bring.

That having been said, my family called in the troops when it really got too much for them to look after us – aunties and

It wasn't a proper adventure unless we got chased.

uncles we never even knew we had. Auntie Rene down the road was no blood relation (we called everyone Auntie and Uncle) but she would shout for us to come over to her house and we'd help her make bread and cakes and devour saffron buns as big as tea plates. Her husband, Uncle Jack, was also kind, though in my very early years he didn't make much of an impression on me – at least until my father died.

The most important thing in any family is having stability, an anchor. If you have nothing in life to hold you in place, you're like a ship at the mercy of the tides: you could end up drifting anywhere. And that would have happened to me, if it hadn't been for a packet of lettuce seeds.

The war took its toll on Father and I believe, really, that was what finished him off. When I was eleven, he finally succumbed to the illness he'd been struggling against for years. When you're young, you don't really realise when someone's sick, how bad they really are. Until, one day, you wake up and Father's gone. And then you cannot accept the fact, because you barely appreciate what day it is, let alone something as permanent as death.

I remember being taken upstairs. The curtains were drawn and the bedroom was dark and smelled musty. Father was lying still in bed. I thought he was sleeping and went to shake him to wake him up and Mother said, 'Leave him be, John. He's dead.' And I just said, 'Why's he dead?' She hadn't an answer to that. No one had.

I could not accept it, because I didn't know what the word meant. Children weren't expected to go to funerals, but I went. I watched him being lowered into the ground and all I was thinking was, Why have they done this to my father? I didn't know who 'they' were, just that they were responsible. It was the lowest point of my life.

With my father's death, my carefree days in Cornwall came to an abrupt end. Mother was left to care for all of us, and she was simply unable to manage. It was 1952 and the prospect for children who couldn't be looked after properly was terrifying: life in an orphanage, where little ones seemed to be punished for not having parents! Mother, bless her heart, tried her best, but she just couldn't cope.

An official came round and declared, 'The children will have to be put away.' I remember hearing this prim and proper lady with a particular accent talking about us like inanimate objects, as though we weren't there. My world felt as if it was caving in. I became empty and isolated because I feared I'd be taken away. And, when you're little and no one is telling you any different, that fear multiplies a thousand times over.

The innocence of my previous life disappeared the day Father went below ground. But behind my fear was an edge of defiance. I could be a determined little bugger when I chose, and I immediately decided I would go out to be the breadwinner of the family. I began doing odd jobs in the hope that it would help keep my family together and me and my sisters away from the orphanage. All the defiance in the world wouldn't have helped without adult intervention, though, and my saviour came in the form of Uncle Jack. He was Rene's husband and he was a big man (probably because of all the huge saffron cakes, I thought). He wasn't happy with what was going on, so he stepped in and said, 'I'll look after the boy.'

I don't remember the detail, but the authorities backed

THERE'S METHODIST TO MY MADNESS

off for a while and suddenly life took on another gear. Uncle Jack would knock on my door on a Saturday morning and say, 'C'mon, boy,' – it was never 'John' – 'you're going to football today.' I started visiting different places. I'd get on the steam train to St Austell, St Blazey and Truro with a pasty and a bag of buns and cake. I'd lean out the window, the coal dust in my face and the steam blowing by. It was so exciting and it seemed as if the whole world was opening up again. But, more than anything, it was the kindness and absolute patience of this gentle giant of a man that helped me through a dark phase of my growing-up. His simple, straightforward, want-nothing-back generosity of spirit in a very uncertain world had a profound effect on me. It made me resilient and it made me believe that not only was the world worthwhile, but that I had a meaningful place in it, too.

2

Spades and Alchemy

One crisp morning, quite soon after my father had passed away, Uncle Jack turned up on our doorstep wearing wellies and tatty trousers held up with braces. He was holding a Cornish shovel. I looked up at the handle, which was towering above me. 'I hear from Aunt Kath you like flowers.' In between feeding myself cake from Auntie Rene, I had often ended up at Aunt Kath's little detached cottage surrounded by rosebushes and chrysanthemums. It was an oasis of tranquillity that drew me whenever the chaos seemed to be building too much. She had a florist's in Newquay and had taught me the bare basics of floristry, after I'd shown an interest in the different varieties.

'Well,' Uncle Jack said, 'let's get you growing things, instead of just cutting them dead at the stems.' He thrust the spade into my hands. 'This is yours now. A bit big, though. We'll have it cut down.'

THE NATURAL GARDENER

My first spade

Right up to 1954, food was rationed. However, the Dig for Victory campaign that had helped feed the nation during the war also left a strong legacy of self-sufficiency, especially for families in rural areas, where living off the land had pretty much always been essential anyway. People had chickens in their back gardens and barter was often the best currency. Swap a hen for a bag of potatoes, fix my leaky tap for a dozen eggs. The difference for us now was that it was government-encouraged.

Jack took me down to the local allotment, where he had a plot. Throughout my childhood, I'd seen men leaning on shovels and admiring bonfires and talking about things I didn't know about. But I'd never been allowed in – until now.

'You've got your spade. Here's your patch.' And he gave me a piece of his garden, just like that.

SPADES AND ALCHEMY

Even after it had been cut down, when I held the shovel upright it was still the same size as I was, but I soon tamed it and started digging. I found I liked it. Turning the soil over, the initial resistance, then with a bit of effort you could transform a weedy, unpromising little scrap of nothing into a lush land of potential.

That's the romantic take on it. There was also the money. Though I'd always give most of my odd-job money to Mother, like all normal children I kept a little tucked away for occasional treats (especially after sweet rations were lifted in 1953). So, when Jack gave me my spade, I had tuppence spare that I'd saved for a rainy day. This time, instead of sweets, I used it to buy my first packet of lettuce seed – 'Unrivalled' from Suttons Seeds. Under Jack's patient guidance, I tenderly placed the seed in an admittedly slightly wiggly row.

'Don't do 'em all at once, boy.'

'Why?'

'Two reasons. First, if you mess up you've still got more seed to try again and take learnings from your mistakes. Second, a man, no matter how hungry, can only eat so many lettuces at a time.'

So I saved half the pack for the next planting.

I watered and nurtured and watched them grow into a dozen great beauties. I heard a few rumblings from others on the allotments: 'beginner's luck' etc. Jack congratulated me on the crop. 'You'll be a rabbit by the end of the week with all that lot.'

I liked my greens, but not that much. I had other plans for my produce and I sold my first crop of lettuces fresh for a few

THE NATURAL GARDENER

My first dirty dozen

pence. I'd already made my money back and there were loads more coming. The man I sold them to was Mr Sleey, who had two fruit-and-veg shops in Newquay. When I left him the first time, he said, with a smile behind his eyes, 'If you've got any more bring 'ey down but try cutting 'ee from the bottom rather than halfway through.'

I felt like a millionaire. The miracle of tiny seeds turning into great big greens was matched by transforming pennies into silver! All for just watering the ground and listening to the advice of someone I admired anyway. I reinvested the money in more tools and seeds. Then I kept pestering Jack for more space, until I pushed the pestering up the line and badgered the local council to give me a full plot to work. They agreed, keen to encourage young growers, and, before my eleventh year was out, I had my very own allotment.

The old boys were thinking, *Who's this young whippersnapper?* But I didn't want to annoy them. I just wanted to get on with things. So I offered to be their gopher, fetching water and tools and running down to the shops and supply centres for them. They soon realised I was serious about this gardening game.

SPADES AND ALCHEMY

And I was. I saw it as an escape and an adventure. And, to make the most of it, I had to grow up overnight. My mates were still out playing, still being chased by farmers, and they kept asking me to join them. But now I was getting my hands dirty for a reason, for an end result, growing stuff that could feed my family – and other people's.

Enthusiasm spurred me on and made me confident, but I soon learned to know my place – in a good way. I was surrounded by older, wiser people and, though I was young and impetuous, I knew that I needed to learn from them. So I forced myself to be patient, to consider my surroundings, and generally avoid making a nuisance of myself. I didn't butt in when they were talking: I just stood on the edges of the conversation, listening and picking up loads of tips, many of which I still use today.

To encourage me (and just maybe hoping to put me in my place), the old boys and Uncle Jack urged me to enter the Newquay Chrysanthemum Show. This is a 170-year-old annual event showcasing not just flowers but all manner of produce from growers and farms in the region. 'C'mon, boy, gotta put something in the show.'

I had a little row of yellow turnips, tennis-ball-sized, with taproots in the ground. I pulled them up, cleaned them and put them in the show, imagining the rosette with a big '1st' stuck against my entry. When the judges came round, they smiled, briefly noted my offering and walked on. Obviously, I didn't win a thing.

It broke my heart. Uncle Jack, typically, saw the bright side. 'If you'd won, boy, you'd have been so cocky, nobody would have lived with you. So a good thing.' That was my first connection with the show. I'm now, at the time of writing, seventy-four and I've been involved with it ever since, as a grower, showman, judge and committee member.

Thanks to Uncle Jack and Auntie Rene, the threat of 'the institutions' had receded and it gave my family time to regroup. I went to Jersey for a couple of weeks to stay with my gran. She lived in a cottage and had twenty-two nanny goats and one billy on common land. During the stay, I met my extended family: more uncles and aunties and distant relatives. For a few days I stayed with Uncle Bill in his cottage at St Clements. It was grandiosely called Washington Lodge, and I remember waking every morning to a dawn chorus of frogs from the well in the back garden. Uncle Bill had a big market garden on the island, with tomatoes and early potatoes, and he seemed always to be doing some sort of business.

One morning when the sea was almost flat, he said, 'Do you want to come for a boat ride with me?' We got into his rowing boat and set off. And then kept going, and going and going. The island disappeared over the horizon and then suddenly I was rowing into light surf again with a beach behind me. The boat crunched on the sand and we both stepped out. There was no one and nothing around except for a dilapidated little beach house higher up in the dunes, out of which stepped a tiny old man dragging something behind him. Over my shoulder I heard my uncle bellow what sounded like 'Toolah?' to which the old man simply nodded and carried on towards us.

They ignored me as they started talking at length, and it immediately hit me that I was in France. The conversation rose and fell accompanied by much hand waving, until the

SPADES AND ALCHEMY

man went, leaving a large sack behind him, which we hefted into the boat. I was desperate to ask what was in it, but my uncle's silence warned me off. To this day, I've never found out what it was.

My time on Jersey changed me. The feeling of holding Gran's hand the first time we walked across the common to milk the goats, the discovery that so many of my family were leading interesting, different lives with different futures – it restored my sense of belonging. I'd found my anchor again. Later, I traced my mother's family back to 1500s. They originated from Belgium, then moved to Normandy, then moved to the Channel Islands. For hundreds of years they'd been food produces, market gardeners and growers. So, I never had a choice, really. Growing was in my blood.

When I returned to the mainland in 1954 from my holiday, I saw the world in a different light. I'd glimpsed a solidity that I could have, too. I came home with a sense of purpose and an enthusiasm that could never have happened were it not for Uncle Jack's intervention.

Very soon I had four allotments. Two veg, one fruit, one chickens and eggs. I was fourteen by then and loving every minute of it. From that day to this, I've never really known the price of vegetables, except to sell on to producers in the trade. I grow everything myself. If I want something I just pull it out of the ground. Within an hour, it's on the plate. Cooked simply and tasting perfect, thanks to my wife, Olive.

I kept the allotments going until I had to start work in the big wide world. To be honest, I'd never been a great lover of school – I just wanted to be in the open air, not stuck inside in a stuffy classroom learning about what's outside. What was the point in that? My learning ground was the allotment.

When the time came for me to leave school at fifteen, like all the other kids, I had to go up in front of headmaster for the final bit of advice aimed at preparing me for the future. This is how it went:

'Harris, you're useless.'

'Thank you, sir.'

'Only thing you're fit for is brushing the streets.'

Teachers were cruel then. We had one teacher who, if you didn't answer correctly, would throw the wooden blackboard eraser right at you. I got good at ducking. Another would tweak your ears if you were caught looking out of the window. I had constant earache. This was all pretty standard, but the thing that I still don't get, and that still seems very wrong to me, was that if you had only one parent you were looked down upon. As though it were the child's fault, as though they'd somehow lost a mother or father through carelessness. Nor was it my fault that, when I was very young, we had only one pair of hobnail boots and I had to share them with Mervyn Rickard, son of the next-door neighbours. We used to do everything together – even share hobnail boots! For a while, this meant we had to take it in turns going to school.

And then there was the built-in snobbery: the kids of the parents with businesses were treated better. It was assumed that, if your parents were successful, you would be too. If your parents did menial jobs, why expect anything else for yourself? The message was always the same: know your place.

Well, I did know my place. It just wasn't the same place as

my headmaster had in mind. It was on the other side of the windows I'd been gazing through for the past five years.

'I'll arrange with the council to get you a brush.'

I had to thank him through gritted teeth.

And that was it. No goodbye, no warm pat on the back. Just the door and the word 'Next!' at my back.

I cried all the way home. Then kept crying that evening because Mother was very upset with me. She said it was all my fault, and that I had spent far too much time on that blasted allotment instead of learning my three Rs.

Then I heard that somebody was looking for a boy at a local market garden in Polwhele. I left school on Friday afternoon; on Saturday morning I walked four miles and asked for a job. They took me on.

First wage: £1 19s 1d (about £1.95) for a forty-eight-hour week.

My own lettuces would have to wait a while.

3

Meet the Head Gardener

In most areas of life, I've found the really successful people share their knowledge; they don't waste effort protecting it. But when I was growing up head gardeners were known as a suspicious, officious bunch. They wore bowler hats and key chains and they dictated to everybody. They were petrified of explaining too much because they were so competitive with other head gardeners, and protective of their positions. After all, if you helped the people below you too much, they might topple you.

The head gardener at Polwhele, Noel Masters, was the complete opposite of this. He was one of the most respected horticulturalists in Cornwall at the time and he was a wonderful tutor, who always had time to help other people. Like my uncle, he was a big, gentle man who never raised his voice. Unlike my uncle, he had suffered terribly in the German POW camps. He never talked about it very much but he was a Methodist man, which maybe made him ponder how humanity could act like that. He went in as a big man, came out skin and bone. Just a shadow of the man he was, people said. He treated me like a son.

I was the only one who stuck out a full apprenticeship. The others came and went because the money was poor. There were bigger adventures and fatter wallets to be had in the building trade, as new housing estates sprang up like knotweed across Britain to meet huge new demand. I didn't love my wages, but I did love the work. (I stuck out my five-year apprenticeship. My reward was proper horticultural qualifications and a set of stainless-steel gardening tools – trowel, hand fork and secateurs – forged by the resident blacksmith on the estate. I still have the trowel and use it every day.)

Noel and I took to each other like carrots and marigolds (*see* Chapter 17: 'Friends and Enemies'). He was probably only about forty-five, but he looked ancient to me, his face fashioned by the constant softening of the Cornish mizzle and the battering of the Cornish winds that inevitably follow. More than anything else, he had time for me and I was lucky that he took the idea of apprenticeship seriously instead of using it as an excuse for cheap labour. I often wonder what would have happened if I hadn't heard about that job. Would circumstance have contrived to push me towards the same destination via a different path? All I know is that he saw in me an eagerness to soak up experience and knowledge. And I saw in him a whole encyclopedia of stuff I didn't know, but wanted to.

Noel had devoted his life to private service on private estates. Through him I saw remnants of how things were done the old way. For instance, on the estate, they had a lean-to Victorian greenhouse with grapevines inside. But the roots went outside, fed through pipes in the walls, and burrowed into big pits. All of the estate's dead stock was thrown into these pits and covered with peat and compost. The roots were on the cold north side of the building, the stems on the warm south side.

It was the apprentices' job to dig out the pits every year and refill with the dead rabbits, offal and kitchen waste. The blood content from the 'dead stock' was reckoned to be one of the finest things to feed grapes. It was an initiation digging out the stinking metre-deep mess, then refilling it, and it often marked the point that apprentices would start thinking dreamily about applying for work elsewhere – anywhere else.

If the pits didn't get rid of them, then the pipes would normally finish them off. Everything was heated with a massive, creaky, old-fashioned boiler that fed four-inch hot-water pipes around the estate. As apprentice, it was your job to make sure it never went out, and that the pipes stayed pristine. We'd have to scrub out the insides of the four-inch red lead pipes. It was a job that took hours. No matter how hard you scrubbed or what you used, you never seemed able to make any progress. (I silently cheered the day they moved over to oil-fired burners with hot-air ducting.)

Estate gardening was a hard sell to most boys. In a time of full employment, it was difficult to attract good people into a long-hours, low-pay occupation. The Victorian method of estate gardening was becoming both irrelevant and impossible. Estate owners no longer had the finances to employ large teams to preserve the old ways of doing things.

In Victorian times, estate owners could finance their vanity

THE NATURAL GARDENER

The old estate pits were filled with carcasses of vermin found on the estate.

gardening projects, feeding their own family and guests. They had been driven by pride, competing with other estates just to be the best, concentrating on wow factors – big camellias, rhododendrons, early daffodils, radical garden design. Now, a new strain of gardeners was taking over. Classroom-trained and commercially minded, they emphasised profit through mass production.

Because I was in the in the middle of it, I didn't realise it was the end of an era until much later. By the mid-fifties, everything was changing so rapidly. The old estates were breaking up. People coming back from war didn't want that life. And the people who owned the estates couldn't keep them going following the old 'Lord of the Manor' principles. Though the respect was still there, the deference had gone. The First World War had shaken our social system to its roots with working men returning from the front demanding more representation and decent wages.

The Second World War finished the job. This time around, the disruption was accompanied by a massive technological and economic shift. The fifties saw the start of the great aspirational age – we can all improve our lot by embracing the modern. Faster, bigger, better, cheaper.

Nowhere did this seem to be more apparent than in the home. The end of food rationing in 1954 was the catalyst for seismic change, with a huge rise in demand for more convenient food.

The old estates with their hierarchical rules and restrictive connections with the local economy seemed suddenly anachronistic. The more forward-looking estates realised they would have to become much more commercially minded. And Noel Masters, whilst a great traditionalist, was also no fool. He saw where the seeds were growing fastest and adapted Polwhele to survive. You couldn't make a living by living in the past. Supermarkets wanted strawberries on Christmas Day.

I was very fortunate to be hired right at the cusp between these two main eras. The end of the 'Victorian' era and the beginning of commercially driven gardening. It seems strange to refer to Victorian gardening in the 1950s, but the estates were the last great bastions of tradition and, like the large old petrol mowers that straight-lined their lawns, difficult to steer in new directions.

At Polwhele the land was suddenly turned over to mass lettuce planting, and we built one of the biggest greenhouses in Cornwall with thousands of tomato plants in a single greenhouse. Towards the late fifties, as people found they had more disposable cash to spend on frivolous things that actually made them feel happier, the demand for fresh-cut flowers rocketed and, under the guidance of Noel, Polwhele became a sea of beautiful varieties of anemones, stocks (a beautiful perfumed flower) and antirrhinum. We planted 500,000 a year – with an army of ladies hired to pick, bunch and box up for the Truro train straight up to Covent Garden Market, where they sold within hours of cutting. It was a fashion and the clamour didn't last too long. The work was still labour-intensive and the margins were gradually whittled down to nothing, so Noel got out of it and looked for other opportunities.

Noel accepted the change because he had to. He understood that only a select few estates could remain static, relying on private income or public tours. And, looking back on it, I realise he was a man of great vision, way ahead of his time in many ways. So, even though he may not have felt comfortable with it, when the decision was made to go commercial he pursued it wholeheartedly and with real innovation. He was always ahead of the game, trying to get an edge on his competitors, who were often bigger setups with wealthier backers, and always trying out new things to see if they'd stick.

Noel led where others followed, but he never forgot the old ways. He always used to say, 'When I was an apprentice, we did it like this.' And he sounded nostalgic. Amid all this apparent gain, I think he felt, deep down, that something fundamental had been lost. But on the surface, and as head gardener there, he put on a positive, active front. I was fortunate to be there at the heart of this shift between eras, methods and values.

I liked it at Polwhele. So, after my five years' training, I stayed for another ten, working and learning my way up the ranks until I was Noel's deputy.

4

Moons and New Orbits

As a young man, Noel Masters had learned all about the benefits of Moon Gardening, but with commercial pressures had never really been able to put the method fully into practice. During our time together, he'd mention it every now and then, refer to it generally as part of the 'old way' of doing things. But towards the end – I think he knew he was coming to the end of his life – he started giving me old books and articles about the subject, saying, 'You'll be glad of this, one day.' One of his last requests to me, when he was very ill and confined to his bed, was, 'Will you study Moon Gardening for me? Nobody follows it any more, but it's important.'

I said yes at the time, though I wasn't sure how I'd do it. Later, after he'd passed away and as my career progressed, I felt it was my responsibility to find out what it was all about. There were no computers, and it was hard to find references. I made lots of enquiries, dug out articles in libraries and slowly built up a picture not only of who did it and when, but also how widespread it used to be. It seemed to me strange that a practice so widely adopted for hundreds of years had all but disappeared. All I needed was a chance to put it into practice. To see if it really worked.

Soon after that conversation, Noel gently pushed me onwards and outwards. 'I don't want you to go, John, but I think you need to move on and broaden your knowledge.'

Even though I was very happy where I was – though perhaps a little too comfortable – and had so many fond memories of Noel and Polwhele, I knew he was right. Everything in the world comes under the umbrella of horticulture because everything is affected by it. While I stayed under his guidance I realised I wasn't learning about wilderness, about dealing with nature when she's left to her own devices.

With mixed feelings but a definite sense of excitement, I managed to get a job with the local Newquay parks department. It could not have been a more different way of life. The parks were beautiful, some of the trees and shrubs were new to me and the opportunities for new experiences were endless – except that there was absolutely no urgency. 'We'll get to it tomorrow' was the mantra. It was open, it was outdoors, but it felt like a prison. I don't want to be trapped here for the rest of my life, I thought, putting everything off to tomorrow. I stuck it out for just over a year, then a chance came to look after bowling greens and golf courses. I'd always been fascinated by different types of grasses.

Over the next few years I would learn that grasses belong to the same family as corn; there are numerous varieties used for different sports; they're cut and cultivated differently to perfect the surface; football pitches are 1.5 inches, bowling greens 0.5 inches; walking barefoot on the Cumberland turf of a well-kept bowling green is like walking on the smoothest carpet; no matter how careful you were, self-sowing seed such as annual meadowgrass would be brought in by the wind and the feet of birds and animals, and you had to keep on top of it immediately or it would ruin all the work you'd put in. But perhaps the most important lesson I would learn was that, no matter how perfectly I prepared the pitch at Newquay FC, it was never going to get them promoted.

After a few years, I again felt restless. During the course of my work, people had started coming to me asking for advice and help with small jobs. Eventually, I took the plunge and went self-employed. I liked the freedom. I took on a big hotel in Newquay – the Windsor. They wanted the grounds completely revamped. Joan and Bud Start had bought the beautiful old building way back in 1960 and made it their life project to revamp it. I spent two and half years laying out their ornamental garden, rockeries and water features, and building a nine-hole golf course. One of the main attractions was a four-foot-deep-by-sixty-foot-long bank with carpet bedding to celebrate their silver wedding anniversary – 1952–77. All the letters had to be trimmed every week to keep the shape. Now, the hotel has sadly been demolished and replaced by old people's flats – the only original features are the sea views.

After the Windsor, I was asked back to the Polwhele. By this time, Noel had passed away and the place was in a bit of a sorry state. I returned with the brief from the owners to embrace new food-production techniques. With a staff of sixty people to look after on the main market garden sections, I set up a fully functioning garden centre for the Polwhele estate and everything was 'pot plants, pot plants, must have pot plants'. Hanging baskets were a huge trend at the time and I soon found we were doing up to a thousand hanging baskets a season. And we couldn't produce bedding plants fast enough. All the magazines and TV programmes were saying these were a must-have, and to stay afloat as a business you had to move with the must-haves.

I built up the business. It was just like my lettuce selling but on a grand scale. I enjoyed the new challenge, the organising, putting a business vision into practice, then seeing it through. To keep up with the trend towards ornamental work, we shifted nearly all of the production, from food to flowers, until we reached the point where Polwhele had four hundred varieties of fuchsias alone growing in the garden centre. But as time went on, I found myself back in an office more and more each day, working the figures instead of the soil. The isolation began to get to me.

Like the heads of the estates, as a manager in the garden centre game you always needed to be stealing a march on your competition. If you got a new display, within two weeks everybody would be copying you and you'd have to push on again. Once I realised this, I knew that the success of the business rested on planning everything way ahead. For Christmas, Valentine's and Mother's Day, we'd order and set stuff up months, sometimes years in advance. You'd then need to allow for the elements. With a mild winter, plants matured early; with a bad one they came late. We needed to do a belt-and-braces approach to cover as many scenarios as possible.

I enjoyed it, but in the early 1980s I had three heart attacks in three years from the stress of running the centre. After my third heart attack, I'd been forced by work pressures to get back in the office within a couple of days. A ridiculous situation. So I decided it was time to get out. Making money for someone else was not really enjoyable if it was going to kill me.

Always look forward. Adapt to circumstances.

5

Rex the Rogue

Now, there was a crazy old gent, Rex Davey, a true country eccentric and owner of the Tresillian Estate, who always used to come into the garden centre, buying all manner of seeds and produce and tools and the latest fads. It always seemed to be something different. The only constant was the haggling over the price. I used to love his coming in for what was a good, friendly sparring match. One day he bustled into the main shop and, instead of buying stuff, he announced directly to me, 'I'm looking for somebody to sort things out at the estate. It'll be for a few weeks only, but the money's good. Know anybody who'd be up for it?'

His idea of good money was quite different from the rest of humankind's, but I was sorely tempted. I'd been in an office too long, and the stress was going to finish me off, so I replied, 'Me, Mr Rex' (it was never Rex, never Mr Davey, always Mr Rex).

I used to visit Tresillian 'unofficially' as a lad and come back with a few choice apples. Even then, I loved it for its grandeur and the possibility of what it could be. It was a magical place, despite the fact that swathes of it had been too long neglected.

I named my price in response to his medieval starting point. Mr Rex mock-fainted and we found somewhere in the middle. The money wasn't great, but the opportunity at Tresillian was. Mr Rex said to me, 'Only for six weeks, mind. Can't afford you for longer, Harris.'

It was worth a punt. If I didn't like it, or he didn't like me, I was still young enough to do something else. But if I proved to him what could be done, offered him a vision of a different type of future for Tresillian, then I could make good on my promise to Noel and myself and finally put into practice the running of an estate based entirely on ancient, natural techniques.

I turned up on my first day with a spring in my step, but as soon as I got through the entrance I was utterly disheartened. The place was an absolute mess: overgrown, overrun, clearly chaotically managed, fertiliser bags everywhere, tools in all the wrong places, rusting machinery . . . Tresillian had been run by a farming family who had very little gardening experience, and it showed. There were sheep in the old walled kitchen garden and wherever you looked everything was overgrown. Six weeks was barely going to make a scratch – a mere speck of time to make any sort of impression. Things needed taking back right to the beginning. So it could only be a clean-up job, cutting back brambles and making sure it looked as if someone actually lived there.

After six weeks, I was called into the office, my head low. I knew I hadn't even achieved my first objective of making the entrance look half-decent. Mr Rex was genetically incapable of getting to the point quickly. I would learn this later, and come to accept it – he was hardwired that way. He talked about the state of the economy, the problems for great country houses like his trying to make ends meet, etc., etc. (after a few minutes he might as well have started actually saying 'et cetera, et cetera'), and I thought, *If you don't want me, please just tell me.* After half an hour of his waffling in his amiable way, I was about to make my excuses and leave, saying thank you for giving me the opportunity, when he suddenly changed tack.

'Right, old chap,' he said, 'I've been talking to my brother. We would like to offer you full-time employment.' He laid it on as though he were giving me the keys to the kingdom. There wasn't just a plum in his mouth: this time, it was his whole orchard. 'You'll be working for a massive organisation with a venerable history. I hope you appreciate the opportunity you're getting here, and make the most of it.' I knew it was his way of laying the ground for negotiation, but I felt like telling him to stuff it in his plant bed. Instead, I said carefully, 'Tell me what you want.' Because there was opportunity here – starting from scratch meant no legacy. It was an open field, albeit a miserably overgrown one. I needed a blank canvas to do what really needed to be done, otherwise I'd be forever compromising.

'Well, we want you to sort that out for a start.' He pointed through the window at the large walled quadrangle with a gated entrance almost invisible under brambles, stinging nettles and creeping ivy. The doors had deteriorated to the point where they no longer really existed and there was a farm gate leaning up across the doorway to keep the animals in. (We later had to go in with scythes, pulling up twenty-foot self-sown sycamores and rebuilding the walls where the stones had been cannibalised for other uses around the estate.) 'You want me to restore a walled garden that looks like a jungle?'

He waved his hand dismissively. 'You made light work of everything else. It's only a few brambles, Harris.'

'They're not brambles, Mr Rex. They're trees – and they're coming out of the walls.'

'We'll find some help for you to shift it all.'

Mr Rex was an honest rogue. He'd try to convince you all his geese were swans, given half a chance. And he was convincing, because he believed it himself.

But I thought, *This is my chance. Nothing to lose.* So I said, 'OK. This is what I want, then. Everything has to be one hundred per cent organic. You let me have complete control over the restoration and preservation of the garden, including resurrecting heritage varieties . . .'

'Ohhh-kaaay,' he drawled, though he didn't look it.

'. . . and it must be lunar-orientated.'

His face pulled in on itself. 'What does that mean?'

'Planting everything in tune with the waxing and waning of the moon.'

He stared at me as though I'd just started speaking Cornish.

'I'll have to talk to my brother. I didn't know you were going to throw conditions at us.'

I asked him to have a think about it and we left it at that. I wondered whether I'd overplayed my hand, but I realised this was probably going to be the best opportunity I'd ever have to start putting theory into practice. I didn't want to be in a constant battle, trying to slowly introduce new ideas to a resistant owner. Better to be all or nothing from the beginning.

A day or two later, he called me up.

'All that nonsense you were on about the other day.'

'Yes, Mr Rex?'

'Do you think it'll work?'

'If you give it time, and let me get on with it, yes. But don't expect instant success.'

'Oh well, you're doing the job. I'd better let you get on with it, then.' That was his way of saying yes.

He was dubious but curious, so he did what he usually did and sat on the fence. If the project failed, I'd be out on my ear. Any success, he would take the glory.

Once I knew what he wanted, I spent endless hours drawing up a plan of action: what would go where, what would look good, what was needed to make the estate look as it should. The whole idea of running an estate is looking at the whole picture – flowering shrubs, ornamental trees, mature trees, woodland and wildflower areas, ornamentals, flowerbeds, fruit gardens, vegetable gardens, orchards and the general layout and wellbeing of the whole thing. Getting the balance right was crucial. Just because a certain person likes a certain shrub or tree, don't fill the place with them. You need balance both aesthetically and ecologically, to avoid any monoculture that could harm the local ecosystem. And you need to pay attention to the smallest detail, because getting it wrong will come back to haunt you.

For instance, the most obvious of all observations is one we all forget sometimes: when you plant something, it's going to grow. It might look like a little twig when you put it in today but in five years' time it'll be a tree. Many people putting small plants in place them too close together because they forget this basic fact. You end up with the heart-rending decision: which one do I move or, worse, destroy? My philosophy has always been: be your own master; don't be led by the latest trend; and keep thinking a dozen seasons ahead.

6

'The Clearance'

It took two years alone to clear the trees, rubbish and brambles from Tresillian's kitchen garden. That early period was hard, hard work. Everything was antiquated, rusty and worn-out, broken, disorganised or just made no sense. But the potential was huge and I woke up every morning with the same excitement I'd had as a kid on my first allotment.

I was allowed two young lads to help me do the grunt work, and started teaching them all the things Noel had taught me. Knowledge grows only when it's passed on. One of the lads, Dick Cole, is now the leader of the Party for Cornwall, Mebyon Kernow, so his experience clearly taught him determination and resilience for a good cause in the face of overwhelming odds.

The main aim, apart from clearing and organising during that time, was to gradually build contacts with organic organisations, preservation societies and suitable seed suppliers.

THE NATURAL GARDENER

Organic gardening was still its infancy then, and very much seen as a hippy thing, on the back of 'flower power' and Prince Charles talking to his plants. Lunar gardening hadn't even been heard of. So when I first started dealing with the existing contractors with the estate and local merchants, I could sense people thinking, *Not another one!*

But I didn't care. There was something much greater at stake here than personal pride or ego. I was passionate about preserving horticultural heritage. If it grew, we had a duty to preserve it. If a building falls, you can rebuild. But, if you lose a variety of plant, it's gone for ever. And as a nation, as a culture, that's exactly what we were doing. Food was becoming more and more straitjacketed, with many varieties falling out of favour simply because they weren't a perfect green, or smooth-skinned or uniformly round.

Restoring the old kitchen garden.

'THE CLEARANCE'

If we could just get the whole thing together, make our own fertiliser, grow our own feeds and grow plants to make these feeds, then we could show how it could be done – almost completely self-contained and self-sufficient. Our ancestors did this, so why couldn't we? They lived well and healthily and left a positive, or at least a neutral, impact on their environment. I wanted to do the same. But, importantly, now that I had a few decades of commercial experience behind me, I also wanted to prove that you could do this without it costing the earth. Because, if you show people that by doing something differently, against the accepted norm, it helps others but also boosts your self-interest, the argument's won.

The old boy Rex never admitted he liked it, but he started to bring some of his friends around. And when I heard him say one day, strolling through the kitchen garden as if he owned the place, which of course he did, 'This is what I've had done here; it's essential we safeguard our horticultural heritage for our children, and our children's children,' I knew I'd found my place and my place had found me.

Within a year or two of 'The Clearance', as I came to think of it, the walled garden started to come together. We were getting varieties of sweet peas going back to 1699. People would say, 'What a perfume! Never seen them grown like that before.'

The walled garden was a major job. After clearing, we set about hand-digging the entire plot. After a whole winter's hard work, a lot of swearing and a lot of sweat, literally removing barrowloads of unwanted material, the foundations for the new garden were ready. The walls repaired, I had my blank canvas. The job was then to lay out the garden and decide what was going to go where. I measured it so that the herb garden was in the middle, and I found a lovely old birdbath that had been neglected and restored it (it's still the centrepiece). Then I began the process of laying out all the beds along the inside walls.

For the north-facing wall I dug a two-foot-wide trench, and planted redcurrants and cooking-cherry trees. Both thrive in the shade, which keeps the fruit on the sour side, rather than sweet.

On the south-facing wall we saved some very old heritage variety pears and quinces, including a Guernsey Pear tree, which was well over a hundred years old. It had been badly neglected but TLC and good management brought them back and fruiting for Cornwall.

On the east-facing walls there are now trained Cornish aromatic and Cornish gillyflower apples in fan shapes and cordons (upright stems with no side shoots, just spurs coming off the main stem, growing at a 45-degree angle).

On the west-facing wall are further mature pear trees, mainly Conference and Beurre Hardy.

The flowerbeds underneath the trees have been recreated to resemble the original Victorian tradition of allowing easy access, so that the lady of the house could pick her flowers without walking on the soil and getting her feet dirty.

The remainder of the garden is laid out in four identically sized beds, three for food, one for flowers, all rotated (*see* Chapter 14: 'Crop Rotation'). That was the inside sorted.

Once I'd laid out the garden and set the paths, we then

decided what was going into Beds 1 to 4, tested the soil pH and, determining where the better soil was during the big dig-over, we matched plant to optimum soil type before first sowing and planting out.

Around the outside of the kitchen garden are fertile fringes and beds. For the exterior north wall we revived some wonderful old Conference pears that hadn't been pruned for many years, under which we created a mixed border growing rhubarb, gooseberries, whitecurrants, blackcurrants and cold frames for propagation. The east and west borders on the outside are now used for mixed purposes, varying from year to year.

I now had a chance to start saving heritage varieties from around the world on a large scale. It was something I'd been fascinated by for many years, testing out hard-to-find seeds in my own back garden. At the time, EEC regulations were gradually squeezing out many of the old heritage varieties being used on a commercial basis.

During this time we created one of the finest orchards in the county, underplanted with daffodils. Trees were planted in a diamond pattern, each one 27 feet apart. We put them in as whips, grown on our own rootstock.

At first, Mr Rex was adamant this was a waste of space. All these tiny saplings miles apart. I said to him trees are like people: they'll develop and grow. Give them space to breathe and they'll reward you. Within twenty years they'll be touching. But he saw only empty space and a wasted asset and wanted to be doing all sorts between the trees. It was a struggle, but I got my own way.

He was always quoting some 'expert who told me you should do this'. And I was always thinking, *Here we go. Another anonymous person who knows best.* He used to call me into his office and tell me bizarre stuff. Rex was a Home Guard man. You'd think to listen to him he'd stopped the invasion single-handed as a major in the SAS. 'When I was a boy, we'd throw potatoes at each other to practise and pretend they were hand grenades – *boom!* – ha, ha.' I would sit and listen to his stories while the weeds were growing outside.

Throughout the 1980s work continued across Tresillian Estate. A notable example was the Camellia Drive, which, when I arrived, was in name only, with the odd wilted residue of a plant on the verges. Over a few years, we introduced numerous varieties of camellias, magnolias and ornamental shrubs. Today, if you walk the drive, when they're out in profusion, it's a beautiful sight, underplanted with daffodils and naturally seeding wild flowers such as bluebells.

It was in 1990 that the estate was visited by Mrs Thatcher. It was a big occasion for us and everyone was there for the event. The idea was for us to line up, have a polite word and move on. I was last in the queue, but when it came to my turn we just started chatting. Whatever your political take on her, Margaret Thatcher was famous for her presence close-up. When she spoke to you, she made you feel important. Very powerful people seem to have this trait in common. She asked about my work at Tresillian (she'd been well briefed and seemed to know more about me than I did myself). Then we started talking in depth about gardening and her favourite plants and how she found the garden at No. 10 very relaxing – a place where she could walk in peace and clear her head.

As we stood there blathering, it became obvious that her

'THE CLEARANCE'

Meeting Maggie and talking 'green' issues.

entourage expected me to move on and her to be somewhere else more important. But we kept chatting away, for about twenty minutes until an aide stepped in and said, 'Prime Minister, we really must be—'

'Don't interrupt!' The sudden ferocity of her voice sent the aide scuttling away. Mrs Thatcher turned back to me and said, 'I want you to do our garden at Number 10. I'll be in touch.'

Six weeks later she was kicked out and I was never asked again. Maybe Mr Major got his peas from Tesco.

When recession hit in the early 1990s, there were rumblings that the venture was costing too much money and the Daveys weren't generating enough for the estate as a whole. The kitchen garden was just a showpiece, and, though it pretty much paid for itself, it was not essential to survival. Another branch of Mr Rex's business was being dragged in to support it. So in the end we had to lose staff.

But we got through it and we kept pushing on. When the economy turned, the Daveys sold up, and the current owners, the Robinsons, provided the financial stability to keep the project developing for the long term.

7

Tresillian Today

Tresillian House, July 2015

Tresillian Estate is now a fully managed twenty-eight acres of gardens and woodlands. Under the considerate direction of George Robinson, returning to the grand home his parents visited and played in as children in the 1930s, it has been tastefully renovated inside and out. Formal gardens surround the house with lawns and borders leading down to the ornamental lake. All the flowers, fruit and veg from the Victorian walled kitchen garden supply guests of the estate. The orchards are responsible for keeping connoisseur cider drinkers merry the world over because Tresillian is proud to supply organic heritage-variety apples to the wonderful Cornish Orchards cider company.

We are preserving our horticultural heritage seed by seed. We currently grow eighty-six of Cornwall's known one hundred native apples, including the Menacken Primrose, which dates back to about 1804. All of these varieties are close to extinction.

The orchards are just one example of the heritage work that lies at the heart of the Tresillian project. Our heritage seed library grows, records and stores thousands of plants and seeds of yesteryear, where the old varieties would be lost and gone for ever if we did not retain them and grow them in the way they were meant to be grown. And this is the key point. Without establishing our gardens using organic, traditional and lunar approaches, many of these varieties simply wouldn't stand modern ways of cultivation.

Our aim is to maintain the genetic bank of all the old proven varieties of the past that are no longer used. I'm currently growing an onion that was a popular variety in Spain only a few decades ago, but that is now being overtaken by modern seed suppliers.

It's important to note that we are not against modern seed production: we are just protecting against the inevitable economic and ecological consequences of it. When the big seed companies go to the seed auctions, they buy sackfuls of seeds to breed new varieties and hybrids. The aim is understandably always to produce a plant that will blow its competition out of the water. The heritage seeds we look after were made much the same way as those now, but it's just done on a mass scale nowadays. We must never forget that what the superproducers are doing today will be heritage in seventy years' time.

As well as preserving old varieties, we're also breeding new ones, using only traditional methods – a recent example being the resurrection of the Summercourt daffodil, originally bred by George Robinson's grandfather in the 1930s. I also bred two geraniums, Cornish Red and Kernow Rose, for the millennium.

When I set out on this path at Tresillian back in 1984, interest in organic and natural food production was only just beginning. Now, I'm delighted that, wherever you look, restaurants and growers emphasise local produce, eating food that's as fresh as possible, embracing local varieties and ways of cooking. There's been a real artisanal food renaissance in the UK in the past twenty years. It seems we're all rediscovering old cheese recipes, growing wines, celebrating our diverse and wonderful culinary heritage. How we put our seeds into the land and take our food out is all part of it.

I believe that our kitchen garden and estate would not have achieved their considerable success had I not been allowed to follow the ancient principles of planting, pruning and harvesting to a lunar calendar. I've spent most of my adult life outdoors at all hours watching nature, and I have become utterly convinced that the moon has a huge effect on all living things.

There will always be sceptics. That's fine. But all I ask of anyone is go into any subject with an open mind. I've learned so much from people I initially disagreed with. Now, if someone's going to make a point, I try to stand back and actually listen to them. Too many discussions are simply two opposing viewpoints repeating long-held assumptions without ever even entertaining the other point of view. I think real learning comes by empathising with the opposition. By empathising, I don't mean agreeing with, necessarily. I mean by genuinely trying to understand where that viewpoint is coming from. Only then can you truly evaluate it against what you already currently know and believe.

Which is why I fully accept that life moves on. If we didn't move on, we'd all still be wearing bell-bottom trousers – and then where would we be? (Thankfully, bell-bottoms passed me by – they would've just flapped around my wellies gathering mud, anyway.) Point is, even though we're maintaining an ancient and traditional way of life at Tresillian, and I'm an advocate of organic and lunar gardening, it's not because I have an axe to grind. I have upset some of my most vocal ambassadors in the past by saying this, but I'll repeat it: I've never been 'against' modern methods. Chemical fertilisers and mass production have their place. The world needs feeding – and technology can help us achieve that. However, in the pursuit of the new, we have come perilously close to losing heritage breeds of all manner of plants, along with the valuable knowledge of our forebears.

Just because it's old, it doesn't mean it's out of date. Just because it's new, it doesn't mean it's evil. I want to show how you can provide for yourself and your family, using techniques that work in harmony with nature and with nature's support. Some of those techniques just happen to be thousands of years old and rarely written about elsewhere.

SO, TO MOON GARDENING

What's this potted history of my life really got to do with Moon Gardening and you? Everything and nothing.

Nothing specifically – you haven't yet learned about the phases of the moon and how they affect the growth of plants, but I hope you have taken from this so far the benefits of keeping an open mind. I was fortunate to have been taught by Noel Masters, one of the UK's most talented commercial horticulturalists. He pursued what works with vigour, never letting his prejudices get in the way of a juicy radish.

And everything? If I've learned one thing in my gardening life, it's that everything is connected. Not necessarily in some mystical way, but practically. Gardening is all about cause and effect, empirical observation, building your knowledge and applying it all to the way you work. A lifetime of trial-and-error-filtered knowledge is worth passing on – and the wonderful thing is that, every time it is passed on, it's adapted, augmented and reshaped for a new generation.

What's happened in my life and the many precious people who have filled it to overflowing have obviously shaped my career, as with anyone else. But I do feel uniquely privileged that, at my very lowest point, someone down the road shoved a spade in my hand and said, 'Dig!' And that a different someone actually bought my first ever wiggly row of lettuces, revealing to me the double alchemy of horticulture. And that the first job I ever had demonstrated, in practice, techniques both ancient and futuristic under the tutelage of a horticultural genius. And that, when I got my big chance at Tresillian, the owner, probably against his better judgement, trusted me enough to indulge my experimental lunacy. And, finally, that my wife Olive, among her myriad virtues, makes the best flaky pastry Cornish pasties bar none (yes, even better than your mother's), from chuck steak, onions, turnip and tatties – and never, ever carrots – using the veg from our garden only a few steps away. Because that, in the end, is what it's all for.

Gardening has been my solace, my passion and my escape. The life lessons I've learned outside of horticulture I have applied to specific techniques in the garden, and what I've discovered by watching abundance sprout from previously arid ground through a little love, nurture and patience, I have tried to adopt in all areas of my life.

The surprising influence of the moon has just made it all the more fertile – as you're about to find out for yourself.

Part Two

Harnessing the Power of the Moon in Your Garden

How to grow more and better for
less effort and cost

8

The Rise, Fall and Rise of Growing Your Own

During the Second World War, encouraged by the Dig for Victory campaign, growing food for yourself was normal, in many cases a necessity. The legacy of this in the late forties and early fifties was an allotment patch in every village and every town or city neighbourhood. By law, every local council outside of London was – and not so many people know this, but still is – required to provide allotment provision where none exists.

Then the allotments began dying out. The postwar push for modern and fast saw the rise in convenience food, out-of-season produce and supermarket dominance along with a corresponding disconnect between the food we ate and knowledge of how it got to our plates.

Now, thankfully, the tide has turned once again. People are begging to grow their own. They want to feed themselves, and taste food that has a connection to the soil it came from. This shift became more pronounced after the 2008 global financial crash, when the idea of cheap, plentiful food was brought into sharp relief. But the move towards real food provenance started much earlier. There has been an artisan-led British renaissance in the past couple of decades. You see it everywhere. The lie of drab British cuisine has been exposed as micro-cheesemakers, brewers, winegrowers, fruit-and-vegetable heritage revivalists, traditional meat curers and the like have popped up in their thousands across the UK. We see village craft fairs with tables full of homemade pies and preserves, farmers' markets bringing amazing delicacies to urban centres, and restaurant chefs who now need to pursue the mantra 'fresh as possible, local as possible' almost by law, if they are to succeed. Old traditions are being revived, the bounty of the land and seas on our doorstep rediscovered and celebrated.

You can't get much more locally produced than your own back garden or allotment patch. So, if you're lucky enough to own one, have the decency to make the most of it. You'll benefit from greater variety, know exactly where your food comes from, and relish the knowledge that you've plucked it from the ground with your own hands.

BETTER BY NATURE: TIP #1
How to apply for an allotment

Expect a waiting list. Ask your local parish, town, borough, city or district council. If there are none in your area, you have the law behind you. Under Section 23 of the 1908 Small Holdings & Allotments Act, you need a minimum of six people to make a formal request and your council must provide. More details at the National Allotment Society's website: http://www.nsalg.org.uk

9

It's All About the Soil

We tend to take for granted the soil we walk on, excavate, build on and grow from every day. For most people, it's just there. We know but don't think about the fact that it's responsible for pretty much all land life on Earth – and always has been. Natural forces have done a great job of sustaining and developing a myriad species for millions of years without our help. Left to its own devices, natural-state soil nurtures a chaos of life in a complex, sometimes fragile, system of interdependencies.

But the engine behind the chaos is rooted in the simplest of basic rules: cause and effect. If a certain plant grows, another may fade away because of it, or thrive alongside it; or certain combinations of plants may encourage different animals, insects, microbes and nutrients to flourish or flee, above and below ground, which in turn triggers another readjustment of this precarious but often ingeniously self-healing ecosystem. From this frenzied tangle of life, our species' natural instinct has always tended towards controlling the process, instilling order on our terms and to our benefit.

As I briefly describe in Part Three, across the globe from cultures as diverse as the Native Americans and the Australian Aboriginals, our ancestors knew that nature provided when looked after and respected. It was a knowledge built up over many generations, maybe instinctively, maybe tied in with religious and mystical beliefs, too. But it was always fine-tuned and backed up through good old trial and error. Many of the ancient gardening and food-production techniques work, because they had to work. Families needed to be fed from a handful of seed. Knowledge was preserved and built up, passed on from generation to generation, and good advice was sifted from bad in what you could call a natural selection of gardening tips!

The point is this. Treated well, encouraged towards its optimum natural state, soil has enormous potential to feed us with abundant, cheap and varied supplies of stunningly tasty food. And the way to treat it well is to harness the helpful power of nature while taming its love of creating a big mess in your garden.

In this section, I will show you how to get the most out of the soil using the phases of the moon alongside select techniques all aimed at improving the biology and activity of your soil, encouraging good growth and discouraging bad.

10

The Four Quarters of the Moon: Overview and General Principles

Dark moon, waxing, quarter-, half-, gibbous, crescent, light, waning … the various names given to the moon phases often cause confusion. The dark (or 'dark of the') moon is an old term for the new moon, which is hardly ever visible as it sits between the sun and the earth. As the moon moves through its first quarter, a waxing crescent (once called the increasing moon) takes us to the point at which we see half the disc, which we call the half-moon (even though strictly speaking it is only a quarter of the moon). The waxing gibbous sees us through the second quarter to the full moon, which used to be known as the light moon. The full moon is followed by the 'decreasing moon', as it was called – waning gibbous as it travels through the third quarter, and on to the fourth quarter, through a waning crescent back to the (dark) new moon – full circle!

THE NATURAL GARDENER

THE MOON CYCLE

The moon month is made up of four quarters over a twenty-nine-day cycle, three quarters of seven days, one of eight, changing from month to month. Though various systems give them different names, throughout this book I've just named them first to fourth quarter with new moon at the start and full moon halfway through. Other versions of Moon Gardening are more concerned with signs of the zodiac and the positions of the stars. This is a very different approach, not to be confused with the one I've developed at Tresillian. I like to keep an open mind, so I am neither endorsing nor rubbishing other viewpoints. I just follow what works, and I know that the Tresillian version of Moon Gardening works!

The first day of the first quarter is new moon, when the moon is not visible in the sky. At this point, the strength of the moon's gravitational pull on Earth is at its weakest. The pull increases from this low point throughout the first and second quarters. By the end of the second quarter (full moon) and at the start of the third, the gravitational pull is at its strongest.

As soon as the third quarter begins, the strength of the pull begins to fade. It keeps ebbing throughout the third and fourth quarters until you reach the end of the fourth quarter, by which time you're at new moon again.

Earth's water table responds to this never-ending rise and fall of gravitational pull. It rises as the moon's gravitational pull increases and it falls back as it decreases.

THE FOUR QUARTERS OF THE MOON: GENERAL PRINCIPLES

WHY THE RISE AND FALL OF THE WATER TABLE MATTERS

When the water table rises it exerts upward pressure. The moisture beneath your garden soil rises with it. This increases the concentration of moisture content at exactly the level in the topsoil, where we gardeners do our gardening.

This unfailing act of nature will carry on until the moon stops orbiting Earth. It is of great help to us, especially during periods of low rainfall in the summer, but with careful and aware gardening you can benefit throughout the year. Here are several key activities which are heavily influenced by the lunar cycle:

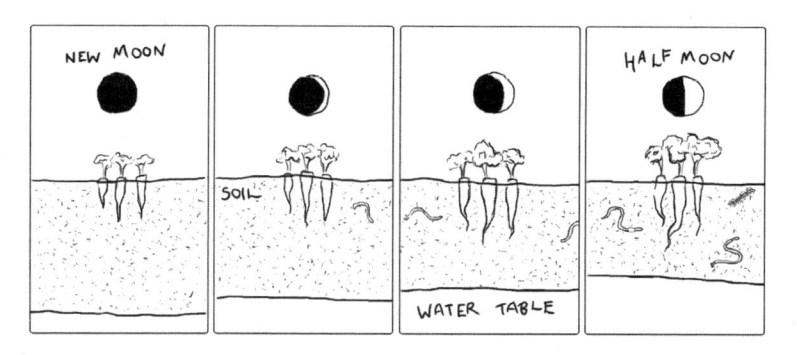

As the moon waxes in the first quarter, its gravity pulls the water table up; this in turn encourages increased soil activity.

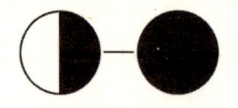

THE PRE-WINTER DIG

If you follow the crop-rotation programme described later, you'll be 'manoeuvring' and fertilising your soil well in advance of planting out and sowing in the spring. Even if you don't rotate, this is still worth doing. The autumn dig begins in September, October or November, preferably October, at the start of the moon's fourth quarter in each of these months. The water table has fallen halfway and is still falling. This releases pressure on the dug soil and makes it more receptive to air and airborne higher temperatures.

This combination of 'drawing in', warmth and increased airing encourages increased vegetable-processing activity by the soil's creatures and insects. This sparks a virtuous cycle, which sustains and enhances biological activity, resulting in increased natural fertility.

At this time you need to check your pH and add lime or calcified seaweed to balance the soil. If you find you need to add lime etc., it's very important to remember that you will then have to wait to apply manure until February. There needs to be at least two to three months between applications of lime and manure, to allow time for the lime to work its way through the soil. But, if the soil is balanced, you can put the manure in during the dig to help feed this natural activity. At the same time, at the start of the moon's fourth quarter, the soil, being less moist, is lighter. So it offers less resistance to your fork, spade and hoe.

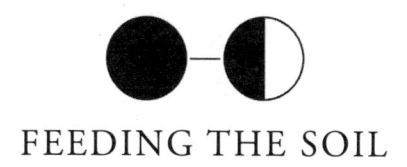

THE FOUR QUARTERS OF THE MOON: GENERAL PRINCIPLES

FEEDING THE SOIL

You want to add nutrients to the ground when it's at its most receptive. This way, you work less, you're more efficient and your costs are reduced. Manure and fertilisers should be worked in at the start of the moon's fourth quarter, as close to the first day as possible. Throughout the third and fourth quarters, the water table is falling, releasing pressure on the dug soil and encouraging more thorough and deeper absorption of any additions to the soil.

Feeds applied during this quarter are drawn into the drier soil and can be applied more sparingly than during other quarters. I wouldn't be able to afford to run Tresillian or my own garden at home without the help of the moon. The moon's final phase sees its pull on Earth diminishing to its lowest point, the water table with it. As the water table recedes, it draws any fertiliser applied to a deeper depth and encourages wider, more even dispersal.

Apart from leaving more money in your pocket, using less fertiliser is great for wildlife and the health of the soil generally, reducing chemical build-up – because every drop of run-off adds to the problem, as any farmer will tell you.

THE NATURAL GARDENER

> ### BETTER BY NATURE: TIP #2
> *Save, save, save*
>
> One of the lesser-known benefits of planting and feeding to the lunar calendar is that it saves on fertiliser, labour, pesticides and all manner of other often non-essential paraphernalia sold hard to the gardener every time they read an article or step into a garden centre. Feeding during my pre-winter dig is a great example. I can reduce the amount of fertiliser by as much as 50 per cent of the manufacturer's recommendation.

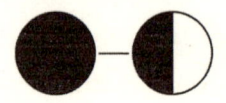

SOWING BELOW-GROUND DEVELOPERS

Sow at the start of the moon's first quarter. Why? For the next two weeks, give or take a day, the moisture content in the soil will be gradually increasing because the water table will be rising. This will combine with the thoroughly absorbed feeds, which you've applied in the previous fourth quarters. This encourages germination of slow developers such as carrots and enhances their survival chances.

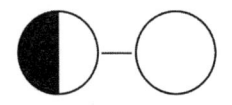

THE FOUR QUARTERS OF THE MOON: GENERAL PRINCIPLES

SOWING ABOVE-GROUND DEVELOPERS

Above-ground developers such as cabbages tend to be fast growers. Sow these at the start of the moon's second quarter. For the following week the well-moistened soil combines with thoroughly absorbed feeds (which you added at the start of the previous fourth quarters). This creates the ideal conditions to encourage the rapid germination that fast developers need both to survive initially and reach their full potential later on.

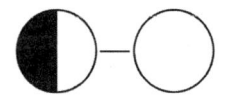

PLANTING OUT

One of my golden rules is that feeds should be added to the topsoil ten to fifteen days before sowing or planting out. This way, your new arrivals get the maximum benefit from the various manures, feeds or fertilisers you add. Planting out can be a traumatic experience for seedlings and young plants generally. Most plants abhor sudden change. That's why, unless you handle things carefully, moving plants from a small pot to open ground can mean they don't take, or they plateau for too long and never reach their full development potential.

For best results, insert young cuttings, plantlets, bushes or saplings into the soil at the start of the moon's second quarter. Thanks to a rising water table, the soil is already getting moister and will keep doing so for roughly another week. This creates the ideal conditions for supercharging plant development. A good tip is to plant in the cool at the end of the day. There's less evaporation, hence greater moisture retention in the soil. The increased pressure on the newly inserted plant's roots, exerted by the rising water table, encourages increased sap flow and, consequently, faster nutrient ingestion from the soil.

I see this situation as the perfect combination: increased moisture, better nutrient absorption and greater sap flow join forces to create the conditions for excellent, healthy growth. Essentially, all plant life is at its strongest and pushing hard for survival at the end of the second quarter and the beginning of the third. Full moon, in other words.

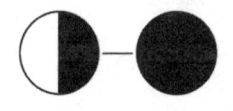

PRUNING

Wherever practical, all cutting back of plants should be done when the moon is in its fourth quarter, the closer to new moon the better, because you want to minimise sap loss. Towards the end of the week before new moon, the water table has almost completely fallen and is exerting no upward pressure. This means less sap discharging from the wounds of your surgical operations in the garden, which means faster healing.

I've seen apple trees pruned at the wrong time. The inserted cut doesn't heal and the chances of disease are much greater. In the Tresillian orchards we treat our apple trees like children. You train them intensively when they're young, but after they've reached fourteen or fifteen years you should then have to give these teenagers only the occasional clip round the ear via a little light pruning. A good pruning rule is to aim to keep the centre of your fruit trees open as much as possible to let light in. With older varieties, this is not always possible because of their twiggy, branchy growth. This is the nature of the beast, so one has to accept the fact that this is how they grow. As with particularly wilful children, sometimes it doesn't matter how much pruning you do, you aren't going to stop them developing what they initially set out to do. You need not worry too much, though. A combination of modern grafting techniques and hybridisation means that most varieties you can buy nowadays naturally achieve the optimum 'open goblet' effect.

HARVESTING: BELOW-GROUND DEVELOPERS TO BE STORED

Remove roots and tubers, such as carrots, from the soil when the moon begins its fourth quarter. At this point the water table is falling towards its lowest level and exerting least upward pressure. This means the topsoil is in its naturally driest state, and so too are the surfaces of the plants you're pulling from it. The drier the root or tuber surface, the less likelihood of rot.

For optimum results, harvest at the end of the day, and transfer your produce immediately into store. By doing this, you avoid exposure to the sun and further drying through evaporation. The result is veg staying as firm as when first removed from the soil.

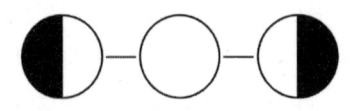

HARVESTING: BELOW-GROUND DEVELOPERS TO BE EATEN IMMEDIATELY

Of course, you can't always wait for those lovely carrots. If you want them for your plate the same evening, the best possible time to pull them from the ground is at full moon, then a few days either side. The water table's at its peak, pressure pushing moisture up into the topsoil to its maximum level and, in turn, inducing the maximum amount of sap in your crop. You are pulling veg out of the ground at its juiciest. More moisture = more flavour.

Once again, for the very best results, harvest in the cool of the evening or even at night. This avoids evaporation via exposure to the sun, retains the sap and keeps the flavour packed in.

THE FOUR QUARTERS OF THE MOON: GENERAL PRINCIPLES

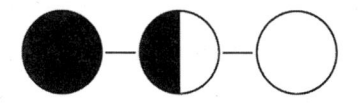

HARVESTING: ABOVE-GROUND DEVELOPERS

Using cabbage as an example, ideally you need to pull leaves, better still the whole plant, from the soil when they're juiciest and most full of flavour. This occurs during the first and second quarters, reaching maximum around full moon, when the water table is pushing moisture high up in the topsoil. In practice, kitchen needs could very well overrule this. Lettuces and cabbages need to plucked when at peak quality and fully mature. There are many variables that will decide maturity, moon phases being only one of them. Therefore, pull them out when you need them and when they're mature. If this coincides with a full moon, all the better.

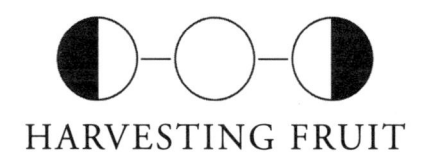

HARVESTING FRUIT

As with above-ground developers, the priority here is pick when they're ready – as soon as they're ripe. Even so, once you start following a moon-gardening calendar, you'll find that the ripest, sweetest and freshest-tasting fruit is at the end of the second quarter and beginning of the third. The water table's at its highest, there's maximum pressure on the tree's roots, and the sap's flowing fullest – all combining to increase flavour.

For all harvesting, it's best to pick fruit in the cool of the evening. This avoids evaporation and ensures your fruit will be in tiptop condition.

11

The Four Quarters in Detail

BETTER BY NATURE: TIP #3

Forget the moon!

Forget Moon Gardening altogether . . . if you're growing in an artificial or contained environment. Plants in pots and containers are not affected by the moon because they have no contact with the water table.

NEW MOON   WAXING CRESCENT   HALF MOON

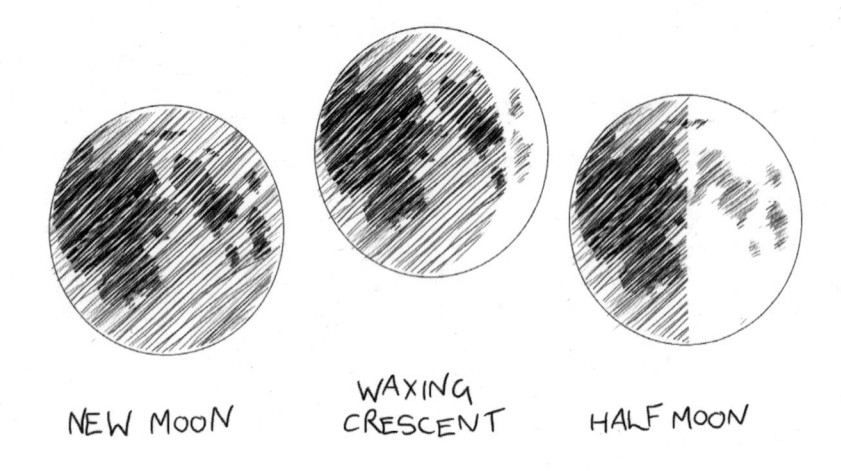

THE FIRST QUARTER

What to do: plant crops below ground

In the first quarter, just after new moon, the moon's influence begins increasing in strength. Slowly, the moon's gravity starts to influence all moisture content on Earth – not only in the sea, but also in the soil.

The more gravity starts to pull, the more moisture starts to come back into the soil that has been drained away over the third and fourth quarters of the previous lunar cycle. The water table is rising, the moisture encourages more beneficial bacteria, the soil becomes more 'active'. This is when all of our plants that produce crops under the soil – e.g. potatoes, carrots, root crops, etc. – are seeking long-term moisture content and will benefit from planting in optimally moist soil from the start. Through practical experience, and systematic trial and error, I've developed this approach for over forty years. It isn't

THE FOUR QUARTERS IN DETAIL

based on mysticism or faith: it's based on the results I see day in, day out.

At Tresillian, the first quarter in spring, when the soil is right and the weather permits, is a wonderful time to be out in the garden – any time in March or April – but if the soil sticks to the soles of your shoes you shouldn't be on it because compacted soil is no good to anyone. There's a surge of energy coming through, the moon's gravity is waking things up – the almonds, peaches, pears and damsons start flowering – and you can almost tell which phase of the moon it is just by looking at the plants around you. Life is starting to wake up and take hold again.

Of course, the unwanted things come to life too at this time of the month – weeds. Remember, though, a weed in a garden is only a plant out of place. Every seed has a use for something in life – it's just not necessarily beneficial to us. However, it's still a part of the ecosystem. I'm not saying be kind to weeds – get rid of them quickly. But, as long as they're annuals and not seeding, pull them and compost them.

Why it works

It's simple, really: the more moisture, the greater the swell in the soil. Moisture makes juice. Juice makes taste. Increase the moisture, get better taste. All root crops planted in the first quarter benefit from the extra moisture and come out bigger, juicier and tasting better – without any artificial aids.

Case history: the 'humble' potato

As an aside: why do we gardeners always refer to the potato as 'humble'? For me, there's nothing superior to creamy, buttery mash made from Majestics or King Edwards pulled from your own patch. It's a far cry from the very primitive potato, probably a sweet potato type, first introduced to our shores in Elizabethan times. The potato is also responsible for one of the greatest social upheavals in modern times: the mass migration of the Irish to America after the potato famine. So it's anything but humble. And, despite its declining popularity in favour of rice and pasta, it's still clinging on to the Number 1 slot for the moment, with billions of tonnes a year grown for supermarkets.

WHEN TO PLANT: Regardless of the month or variety, you always want to plant potatoes as early as possible in the moon's first quarter. But, if you're planting potatoes in an artificial environment or containers, remember the moon has no effect whatsoever, so you can plant at any time.

EARLY POTATOES: 12–14 weeks from planting to harvest. Recommended varieties: Jersey Royals, Arran Pilot, Red Duke of York and Epicure, May Queen and British Queen. All have been grown at Tresillian for many years using lunar-phase techniques. This is just a small sample. There are numerous varieties on the market for professionals and amateurs. See 'Organic Organisations and Resources' later in the book for more details.

MID-SEASON, SECOND EARLY: 14–16 weeks from planting to harvest. Recommended varieties: Maris Bard, Kestrel. You can put these in a month later than your early potatoes, to give yourself a regular spread of potatoes throughout the season.

MAIN CROP: 18–20 weeks from planting to harvest. Recommended varieties: King Edward, Desiree, Cara. These can also be planted a month later than the earlies. At Tresillian, these are our bulk potato, needing a much longer time in the ground, taking us right through the autumn and winter months.

First-quarter checklist

GROUND PREPARATION: This is the time to lightly cultivate the soil. You always want to get more air into the soil. The more air, the easier the moisture table will rise to the top, the better the soil will receive rainwater. It's a good time to get your hoe out because the first quarter is when you'll see the weeds pushing up and beginning to take hold unless you get to them early. The best time to kill a weed is when you barely see it. This way it hasn't been allowed to steal nutrients from the soil intended for other plants.

PLANTING OUT AND SOWING: Everything producing crops under the soil (e.g. carrots, peanuts, sweet potatoes).

HALF MOON   WAXING GIBBOUS   FULL MOON

THE SECOND QUARTER

What to do: plant crops above ground

This is the most important time for planting everything that produces crops above the ground. All cereals, fruit crops and all the flowering plants, including sweet peas such as Old Spice Mix, Cupani (which dates back to 1699) Painted Lady (which goes back to 1730) and a new variety we introduced to Tresillian, King's Scent, which has a wonderful stem length and prolific perfume. Essentially, all the plants that give pleasure to the eye in your garden benefit from being planted in the second quarter.

Why it works

The gravitational pull of the moon lifts the water table, making the topsoil moister. This is the best time for above-ground

THE FOUR QUARTERS IN DETAIL

developers because a flower produces a fruit in the form of a seed pod. It's important that you get the planting done right here, because, the stronger your flower, the better your seed production will be as an end product. This applies to garden peas, beans and sweet peas you're going to save seed from. How often have people gone out to pick peas for Sunday dinner, only to find them underdeveloped because they haven't extracted enough moisture content from the soil? If your plants have been flowering irregularly or disappointingly, this is why. They've been planted at the wrong time of the month and not given the early boost to development they need. As a result, they go to seed too early because they're under stress, and follow their urge to reproduce themselves quickly, so you get no follow-on of flowers.

It's true that developments in new seed varieties have mitigated this problem to some extent, and, because they're designed to work in all conditions, you can easily plant out at other times and in other ways. But I'm taking my cue from the traditional varieties named before, which relied on more careful planning and handling. By following traditional methods, you can guarantee better results, whichever seeds you use.

Planting at the wrong time has a detrimental effect on the growth of the plant, and the grain or seeds it produces. This applies especially to plants that need to be constantly harvested, such as sweet peas.

CASE HISTORY: the sweet pea

Irrespective of whether you grow this household favourite on a wigwam or run a forty-foot row across the garden as we do at

Tresillian, you start them in four-inch flowerpots, early in the year. Note that, when planted in an artificial environment, for example a greenhouse, cold frame or plant pot, the moon has no effect. The body of water is too small to respond to the extra pull of the moon's gravity.

We start the plantlets in November, December and January for continuity of supply, but they are not planted out into the main garden until the phases of the moon are right. As important, though, is that we don't plant out unless soil conditions are right, too. Regardless of moon phase, it mustn't be too cold or growth will be stunted or non-existent.

Beautiful sweet peas in the kitchen garden at Tresillian.

Second-quarter checklist

PLANT: Everything that produces crops above ground, such as corn, peas, beans, fruit and flowers.

Sow: Anything with a short growing life, especially salads right up to August.

FULL MOON   WANING GIBBOUS   HALF MOON

THE THIRD QUARTER

What to do: harvest

The full moon marks the shift from second quarter to third. This is when there's maximum moisture content in the soil because the water table is at its highest point in the twenty-nine-day cycle. This is the time when I go water divining, tracking sources of water for local farmers. It's a lot easier when the moon's gravity is pulling strongest. And this is also when all food-producing crops contain maximum juice and taste. From full moon into the third quarter, plants are extracting maximum moisture from the soil, and with it all the trace elements and nutrients they need. Trace elements to plants are like vitamins to us. If a plant lacks them, things begin to go wrong.

Quite often, people come to me with discoloured foliage

(magnesium or boron deficiency) because, if we've had a very wet spell over autumn and winter when the ground becomes leached by heavy rain, nutrients can be lost or washed away. Where practically possible, the third quarter is the most important time to replenish trace elements lost through flooding.

Why it works

The beginning of the third quarter, full moon, is an ideal time for harvesting many long-storage crops, such as potatoes, apples and onions. In bygone times, the Egyptians would have made sure that their grain was harvested when the heads had swollen to their largest possible size. They knew that, when bulked up, they retain nutrients and moisture better, which aids longevity. (This sounds contradictory, because farmers now use driers to ensure their harvest doesn't rot. But their machines are set carefully not to take too much out and mainly remove surface moisture, i.e. dew, not the moisture within the corn.)

There are exceptions to the above-ground rule. Where you have mass-producing soft-fruit plants such as strawberries and raspberries, which have no prospect of long-term storage, you should harvest and eat them as soon as possible. With such perishable fruit, after a few days the natural process is for it go mouldy and break down. So, if you're fortunate enough to have a beautiful bed of strawberries, harvest them in the third quarter as soon after full moon as possible. They'll taste much better than if you left them for another ten days. Resist the temptation to keep waiting for them to get bigger and better. And remember: if they ripen beautifully before this time due to

THE FOUR QUARTERS IN DETAIL

perfect weather conditions, don't wait till the right moon time. Harvest when ripe.

Supermarkets keep apples and potatoes in cold storage for up to twelve months. Varieties are bred and produced to keep. Non-seasonal supply is a huge business. For the ordinary person with the ordinary allotment, however, the third quarter is the best time to pull your potatoes and pick your fruit. Store them dry and in a dark place and they'll keep for a long time. Not twelve months, admittedly, but they wouldn't last that long anyway: they taste too good!

Case history: autumn veg for storage

Anything that I lift in the autumn for long-term storage I do in the third quarter: potatoes, onion family, garlic and root crops such as carrots and parsnips.

Third-quarter checklist

HARVEST: At full moon pull and pick everything you want for long-term storage such as potatoes, onions, apples and any root veg such as parsnips.

FEED: Prepare to feed all crops that need it after the full moon begins to fade.

HALF MOON   WANING CRESCENT   NEW MOON

THE FOURTH QUARTER

What to do: manoeuvre your soil

The last quarter of the moon's monthly journey is arguably its most important. First and foremost, the moisture content is dropping to its lowest given point. Roughly two thousand years ago, the Chinese were one of the first to realise that cultivation of the soil was done better in this period of the moon's life than any other time, because water is ten pounds to a gallon. They found with their primitive ploughs (the Chinese were also first to invent them) that their water buffalo tired less around the new moon. This was because their work was so much easier. The soil was lighter, the blades slid through the soil with less resistance and, if there was rain, it would disperse more quickly because the water table was lower. The drawing-in action of the receding and bottomed-out water table reduced waterlogging and standing water.

Why it works

The beginning of the fourth quarter is the most important time for fertilising and incorporating all organic matter within the soil because it breaks down easily and nutrients are sucked into the soil and absorbed faster. Organic or dry, the most important thing is to get your natural additives into the ground at least ten days before you plant. This way the nutrients will already have started to break down. (It's detrimental to all plants, especially small seedlings, to sow or plant out at the same time as adding fertiliser.)

Fourth-quarter checklist

The fourth quarter is the restful period so it's an ideal time for getting your garden in order . . .

PRUNE: Clip your shrubs and cut back hedges. The cuts you make will heal more quickly because the moisture content is not rising; consequently, there's less bleeding. (Right up to the First World War, amputation of limbs was carried out in the last quarter based on this – more on this in Chapter 23.)

REPROPAGATE: If you want to increase your stock, irrespective of what it is, now's the time to do it. Separate plants for reproduction purposes because they'll heal so much more quickly. This also applies to grafting.

FEED: While you're manoeuvring the ground, add fertiliser, manures and your liquid feeds (*see* 'Fertilisers, Manures and Feeds' later for detailed advice.)

WEED: Attack those perennial weeds now because there's less chance of their re-establishing.

12

Making Time for the Moon

In gardening, nothing is written in stone. The phases of the moon give you opportunity to extract the most from the soil. They help you eke out extra taste and life from all the natural resources around you. But you can't always follow the rules, because other things get in the way. The biggest ones are the weather and work. We're all slaves to the elements and too many of us are slaves to our jobs. No two years or consecutive seasons are the same, and sometimes the boss takes priority over pulling those potatoes at exactly the right time.

So everything written here is to attain the ideal scenario. If you miss certain things, or you're forced to plant and harvest in the wrong quarters, all is not lost. Just aim at following as closely as possible the moon-gardening calendar and you will see noticeably improved results over the long term.

So, if you're a weekend gardener, or even an every-other-weekend gardener, there's nothing wrong with that. You live in the real world with multiple demands on your time. All the more reason to get as much benefit from the moon as you can, of which the best discipline is good planning. Don't be one of those weekend gardeners who sow all their seeds in one go, then wonder why they end up with fifty lettuces in one week. These gardeners wonder why half their seeds never come up after overfertilising the ground they immediately plant them in. The fertiliser content is so close to the seed that it kills it. (When fertiliser breaks down it releases gas; the young, undeveloped seedling struggles to germinate in the gases, and dies.)

And this particular type of weekend gardener (not you, obviously) says, 'Half of my seeds didn't come up. Not buying from there again.' It's not the seeds: it's the way they were planted. Those lucky enough to germinate suddenly produce a mountain of lettuces and the inevitable end to it all is entreating their friends with, 'Um . . . would you like a lettuce? I have too many.' It's not fair on the lettuce, nor on the garden, nor on the gardener. So take a bit of time to prepare and plan. Be realistic with the number of hours you (and maybe your family, if you can drum up support) can commit to gardening. Then let the moon help you make the most of them

Gardening is all about working out what you want, when you want it, and fitting that into the best time to plant. When gardening becomes a chore, it doesn't work. It should always be beneficial to the person who's doing it and the family it feeds.

13

Superpowering Moon Gardening

A QUICK ASIDE ON CARING FOR YOUR SOIL

In the beginning, the middle and the end, it's all about the soil. As with a doctor, a gardener's absolute rule when treating the land, from which they're expecting so much, should be: first, do no harm. So many of the problems I come across when chatting to amateurs and professionals alike can be traced back to years, decades even, of one well-intentioned gardener after another adding unnecessary feed and medication to the patch under their care.

Always, always be guided by the maker's instructions, or the application levels given here if using your own homemade feeds and fertilisers. There is nothing at all to be gained by giving your plant or crop a bit extra in the belief that more has got to be better. It isn't. Usually, it's damaging, both to the plant you're trying to promote and the soil it grows from. You can always feed less, never more.

COMBINING MOON GARDENING WITH TRADITIONAL AND ANCIENT TECHNIQUES

If you follow the basic principles of Moon Gardening I lay out here, you will see an increase in the fertility of your plants, and you'll notice a taste improvement, too. But, because there are so many variables in gardening, to make the most of the moon-gardening principles, the more you can follow in my guide here, the better the improvement in all areas. That's why you'll see sections here for deep trenching, crop rotation and companion planting, along with vital information on how to feed your garden cheaply and organically.

Of these, I've added deep trenching and crop rotation because they're an intrinsic part of the way we grow at Tresillian and they maximise the effect of the moon. You may not have the time to put these fully into practice, but, if you do, you will not regret it. I urge everyone who reads this, however, to follow the suggestions on companion planting and organic feeding because this is easy to do, naturally promotes healthy growth and reduces unwanted insects without resorting to the pesticides that ruin so many gardens and can completely undo all of nature's good work.

And that is, after all, the whole idea of Moon Gardening and the organic approach, generally. Let nature do what it does best, wherever possible. Harness the power of the sun and moon to reduce your workload and cost, long term. Yes, to realise this fully, there is a fair bit of planning at the beginning of the process and heavy digging at stages throughout; but, once it's all set up, you will appreciate how much you can let the moon do the work for you.

For instance, I have never watered my plants for general irrigation purposes since I started Moon Gardening. Not even during the long drought of summer 1976. I admit that on a smaller scale it may be very difficult for you to follow this, and I make allowances for it in my instruction, but the principle remains the same: using the moon's gravity to your benefit will mean you have to do less watering; will mean the heavy work is easier when you do it at the right time; will mean the harvesting will be more fruitful. So you're getting more out of the soil for less overall input and effort.

HOE, HOE, HOE

Underpinning everything – and I cannot emphasise this strongly enough – is the importance of cultivation throughout the calendar year. The more disturbance you do to your soil, the more it activates the bacteria and fungal spores. Soil is a fantastic, living, changing organism that develops with care. And the best way to keep it aerated, healthy and lively is via your hoe. It's an underused tool nowadays, but for me it's the most important one in my shed.

A good general rule to getting good soil is to aim to change its colour from lighter to darker over time. The darker the soil, the more warmth it retains. Warmth is the key to fertility, germination and better plant life. Add decomposed vegetable matter, mulched, then turned in during the moon's third and fourth quarters. And, if you want to follow the Victorian ways, add soot from chimneys and your fire. That's how Granddad achieved that lovely rich, dark-brown loam and tilth that enabled him to feed his large family right through the year.

14

Crop Rotation

Rotating our crops has been around almost since mankind first started to settle and cultivate the land. As far back as 6000 BC, farmers in the Middle East alternated planting between pulses and cereals. According to the Old Testament, God told Moses that the land was to have a sabbath every seventh year, and basic rotation along the lines of food, feed and fallow is extensively referred to in Roman literature. Though not strictly crop rotation, Native Americans interplanted corns, beans and squashes according to the Three Sisters system (*see* Chapter 21, 'Native Americans and the Three Sisters Method'), because they had learned that some plants put nutrients into the soil that benefit others. But it wasn't until the Middle Ages that the practice of three- and then four-field rotation was adopted and refined as the basis for many of the systems advocated today.

For the organic moon gardener, crop rotation is a highly beneficial approach to soil management that meets the fundamental aim of this book: getting more from your land, naturally.

WHAT HAPPENS IF YOU DON'T ROTATE?

Different types of plants attract different types of pests and take or release different types of nutrients and minerals into and out of the soil. If you keep planting the same crops in the same patch of land, this is what happens:

- The same crops in the same areas become targets for pests, meaning many gardeners understandably reach for the pesticides. Effect: non-organic, less tasty, less healthy food.

- Soil nutrition quickly becomes depleted, meaning you have to use more fertilisers to keep it workable. Effect: increased cost, more effort.

- Using the soil the same way every year makes it become more compacted, less plant-friendly and harder to work. Effect: extra effort, for worse results.

By following crop rotation you ensure:

- fewer pests in your garden;
- a healthy soil structure (essential for maximising the moon's effect on the water table);
- spread of soil-borne diseases is kept to a minimum; and
- nutrient depletion is avoided completely naturally.

CROP ROTATION

HOW MUCH LAND DO YOU THINK I HAVE?!

Many gardeners wrongly believe that you can follow crop rotation only if you have vast swathes of land stretching out from beyond your moat to a distant horizon. Not true. Your urban back garden and modest allotment will definitely benefit from it. There are numerous systems out there, but what follows is my own, built up over forty-plus years of research, trial and error. Combined with Moon Gardening, deep and single-dug trenching and companion planting (all detailed later), I've applied rotation to the walled kitchen garden at Tresillian and the results are consistently wonderful and economical: fertile soil, high yield and ripe, juicy produce, harvested at exactly the right time in manageable quantities.

FIRST PRINCIPLES

When you're starting out on this big adventure, plan your garden carefully. Now's the time to talk to your family about what they actually like to eat. My aim for you – and all responsible gardeners should adopt this – is to minimise waste and increase productivity. So there's no point in allocating land to a bunch of salad crops that trigger resigned acceptance from spouse, sons and daughters when they're brought to the table for the third time in as many days. Crop rotation and organic gardening generally encourage variety, not uniformity, so embrace them and get as adventurous as you want to.

THE NATURAL GARDENER

THE FOUR-YEAR ROTATION CYCLE

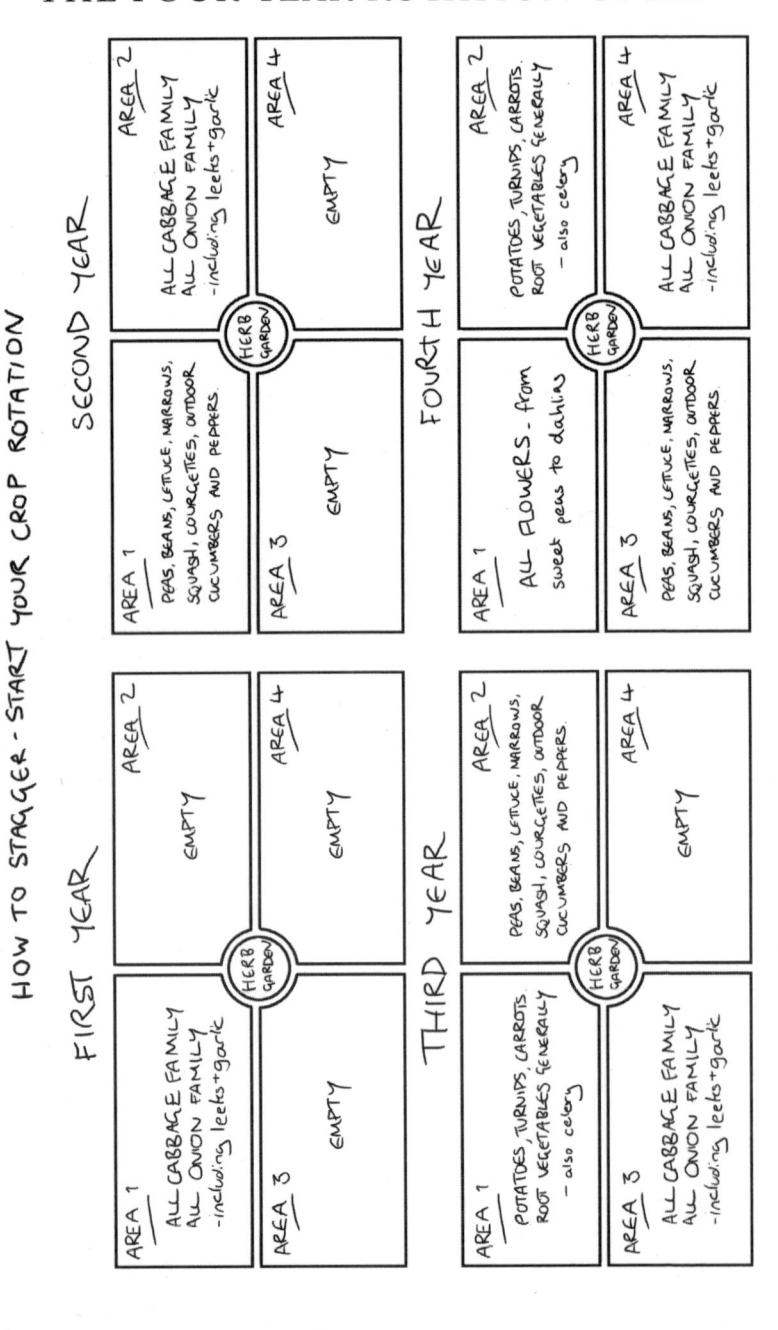

HOW TO STAGGER - START YOUR CROP ROTATION

FIRST YEAR

AREA 1
ALL CABBAGE FAMILY
ALL ONION FAMILY
- including leeks + garlic

AREA 2
EMPTY

AREA 3
EMPTY

AREA 4
EMPTY

(HERB GARDEN)

SECOND YEAR

AREA 1
PEAS, BEANS, LETTUCE, MARROWS, SQUASH, COURGETTES, OUTDOOR CUCUMBERS AND PEPPERS

AREA 2
ALL CABBAGE FAMILY
ALL ONION FAMILY
- including leeks + garlic

AREA 3
EMPTY

AREA 4
EMPTY

(HERB GARDEN)

THIRD YEAR

AREA 1
POTATOES, TURNIPS, CARROTS, ROOT VEGETABLES GENERALLY
- also celery

AREA 2
PEAS, BEANS, LETTUCE, MARROWS, SQUASH, COURGETTES, OUTDOOR CUCUMBERS AND PEPPERS

AREA 3
ALL CABBAGE FAMILY
ALL ONION FAMILY
- including leeks + garlic

AREA 4
EMPTY

(HERB GARDEN)

FOURTH YEAR

AREA 1
ALL FLOWERS - from sweet peas to dahlias

AREA 2
POTATOES, TURNIPS, CARROTS, ROOT VEGETABLES GENERALLY
- also celery

AREA 3
PEAS, BEANS, LETTUCE, MARROWS, SQUASH, COURGETTES, OUTDOOR CUCUMBERS AND PEPPERS

AREA 4
ALL CABBAGE FAMILY
ALL ONION FAMILY
- including leeks + garlic

(HERB GARDEN)

CROP ROTATION

THE CROP-ROTATED MOON GARDEN IN ITS FIFTH YEAR

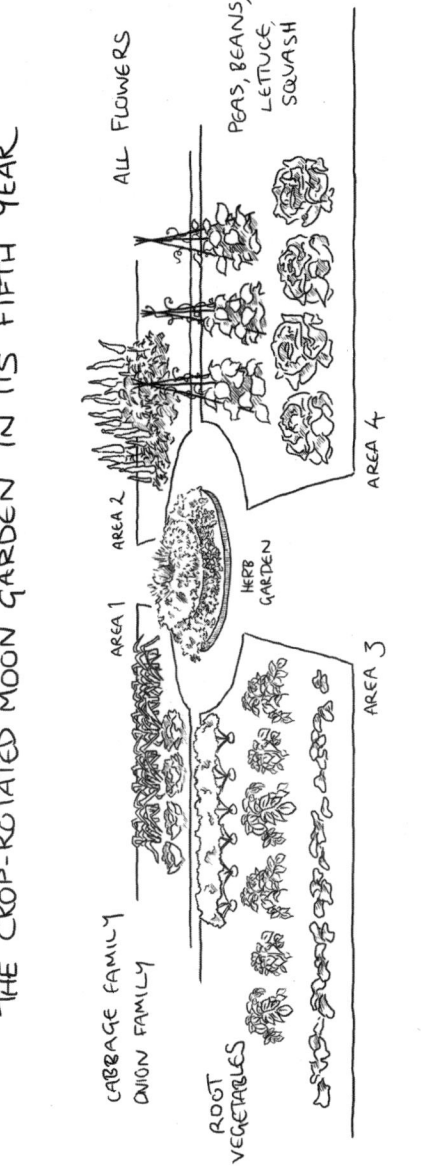

CABBAGE FAMILY — AREA 1
ONION FAMILY
ROOT VEGETABLES — AREA 3
HERB GARDEN — AREA 2
ALL FLOWERS — AREA 4
PEAS, BEANS, LETTUCE, SQUASH

BY THE FIFTH YEAR, THE CROPS HAVE COME FULL CIRCLE AND THE STAGGERED-START IS COMPLETE.

THIS IS AN EXAMPLE OF THE TYPE OF ROTATION YOU CAN FOLLOW BY ADOPTING CROP ROTATION AS WELL AS GARDENING BY THE LUNAR PHASES, YOU CAN SUPERCHARGE YOUR CROPS AS THEY BENEFIT FROM THE RESIDUE OTHERS LEAVE BEHIND.

This is just one example of the type of rotation you can follow. Each new crop will benefit by the residue the previous crops leave behind. Within each area, you can dig different types of bed for different plants.

If you follow these diagrams, it will take four years until the system is fully set up, five till you go back to the beginning. Even if you decide not to take this step, this section is worth referring to for some general growing principles.

For as long as there is a growing season in the year, I use this system to dictate what happens, when and why. The way I use this in the Tresillian kitchen garden is in combination with the deep-trench beds and single-dug beds, described later. They are my versions of the beds of the ancient Greeks and Romans, whose trenches were at least 2 metres deep (admittedly, they had an unlimited supply of slave labour to keep them coming) and filled with sewage and manure from their extensive animal farming. However, in two respects, they have the same essential properties as the ones we use:

1. Trench systems reduce or eliminate entirely the need to water or irrigate.

2. They need a good load of manure and fertiliser to work well.

BETTER BY NATURE: TIP #4
One at a time, please

Warning! Do not attempt to do this all in one go. It may seem like a good idea to create and plant up all four sections of your garden for crop rotation at the same time. It isn't. The four beds must be started one after the

CROP ROTATION

> other, annually, over four years. If they aren't, you'll lose a fundamental reward of the system, because nutrients in the beds will diminish at the same rate. Variety and range come by keeping areas out of step with each other. Besides, you really don't want to be replenishing all four areas of your crop-rotation garden at the same time – a formidable task for even the most dedicated of gardeners.

Start during the moon's fourth quarter, preferably in September before Year One and no later than the November before. This is the optimum month – and time of the month – to lay out your four areas and to begin developing the Year 1 Area. Even though you won't be sowing until spring of the following year, September can usually be relied upon for reasonable weather and soil conditions for bed installation. Over winter, the two bed types you'll be using (deep- or shallow-trench and single-bed, described later) will settle nicely and the surface of the deep-trench bed will smooth over and start collecting rainwater. Watch out for young weeds appearing. Pull them out before you start sowing.

PLANNING FOUR YEARS AHEAD

It sounds daunting but, once you get this going, it can take the stress out of gardening because you know exactly what to do, and when. After a revival programme resurrecting ancient methods in the Tresillian kitchen gardens spanning more than thirty years, I've settled on a four-year system that includes annual flowers. The crops I plant suit the demands of the estate. They may not suit you exactly, but they are detailed here to give you an idea of the variety you can achieve and the thinking behind the system. As long as you investigate which crops should follow which, and make sure that what you plan to grow will benefit from rotation (not all plants do) you can substitute many crops listed here for your favourites.

IMPORTANT: When you start in the first year, you will be doing only Area One. In the second year, you'll be planting Areas One and Two, and so on. (*See* the crop-rotation year planner below and the illustrations on pp. 100–1.)

PROJECT YEAR

	1	2	3	4	5	6	7	8…
Area One	Year 1	Year 2	Year 3	**Year 4**	Year 1	Year 2	Year 3	**Year 4**
Area Two	X	Year 1	Year 2	Year 3	**Year 4**	Year 1	Year 2	Year 3
Area Three	X	X	Year 1	Year 2	Year 3	**Year 4**	Year 1	Year 2
Area Four	X	X	X	Year 1	Year 2	Year 3	**Year 4**	Year 1

CROP ROTATION

Previous page: Note: In the boldface Year 4, you plant and harvest crops as usual for that year, but, by the beginning of the third quarter of September, October or November of that year, you replenish the beds as described in Chapter 15: 'Make Your Bed and Grow In It'. Each area follows the same schedule. Boxed 'Year 1', etc., refer to area years, not project years.

Example life of Area One in the diagram

Note that the crops listed below are not necessarily the same as those mentioned in the illustrations above: they are all suggestions, intending to demonstrate the wide variety of possible crops.

YEAR ONE

Single-dug bed: broccoli, cabbages, cauliflowers, kale, kohlrabi, leeks, onions, peas, savoys.

Deep-/shallow-trench bed: Runner beans, climbing French beans, marrows, courgettes, pumpkins, sweet peas.

YEAR TWO

Single-dug bed: broad beans, dwarf French beans,

Trenches and single-dug beds: dedicated to annual flowers and sweet peas. If you can, plant sweet peas in a deep trench. Normally they flower for a month, but put them in a well-manured deep trench and they'll flower for three months. Lift the tubers and corms annually to safeguard them.

YEAR THREE

Single-dug bed: spinach, swedes, turnips.

Deep-/shallow-trench: potatoes.

YEAR FOUR

Single-dug bed and deep/shallow trenches: beetroots, carrots, celery, parsley and parsnips.

At the final harvest towards the end of Year Four (September–November) the beds are now almost depleted of their nourishment and need to be dug out and rebuilt. Replenish the beds as described in the next chapter, 'Make Your Bed and Grow In It', and start all over again.

YEAR FIVE

The soil has been replenished. Go back to the first year and start again!

BETTER BY NATURE: TIP #5

Feed before sowing

Before sowing, feed the area with the appropriate quantity of fish, blood and bone at the start of the moon's third quarter. Then, below the surface plants, such as roots and tubers, sow at the start of the moon's first quarter. Above the surface plants, such as cabbages and lettuces, sow at the start of the moon's second quarter.

15

Make Your Bed and Grow In It

For making the most of the moon's effect on gardening, I use three different types of bed in my garden. They're detailed here for the enthusiast who wants to take their Moon Gardening to the next level, and they are an essential feature of my four-year crop-rotation system. Deep-trench beds are demanding to dig and not suitable for everyone, so I have included an alternative, the shallow-trench bed, which is not so daunting if you have limited time or strength.

All the beds follow the principles of maintaining and encouraging maximum natural moisture and nutrients from the soil, fertiliser and manures you will be using in your organic moon garden.

Please note, the advice given here for which crops to plant in which beds is based on your first year and first area of your four-year crop-rotation scheme. The 'Crop Rotation' chapter shows you how this develops and varies over the four years. These are for example only, and you can of course choose to plant as you wish. For best results, however, do try to follow the companion-planting principles explained here.

THE DEEP-TRENCH BED

SUITABLE FOR: Sweet peas, runner beans, courgettes, marrows, pumpkins, squashes, often where maximum moisture wants to be retained for the benefit of the crop growing above ground.

WHAT IT DOES FOR YOUR CROPS: The powerhouse of the deep trench is the sponge formed by the bed's layered content of soil and composted vegetable matter. It produces magnificent results because:

- it provides a long-term release of nutrients; and
- it catches and retains moisture from above by its bed's sunken surface and moisture from below by the moon-raised water table; because of this, it doesn't require any watering, even in severe drought.

WHEN TO DIG IT: Beginning of the September, October or November lunar fourth quarter, preferably September, depending on weather and soil conditions.

DIMENSIONS: 1 metre wide x 1 metre deep – length is up to you: you're restricted only by the size of your garden and how much you want to plant. You'll also need to consider how much

MAKE YOUR BED AND GROW IN IT

space your chosen crops are going to take up (*see* Step 2 of 'How to create your first deep-trench bed' below).

WHAT YOU NEED TO DIG IT: Fork, spade, shovel (ideally), two garden lines for guidance and your wheelbarrow to move your excavated subsoil.

CROPS GROWN IN IT VIA ROTATION: The deep trench should ideally make up one part of one of the four areas of your garden that you designate for four-year crop rotation. I use the deep trench as follows:

- YEAR ONE: grow superlative runner beans, climbing French beans, sweet peas, marrows, courgettes and pumpkins.
- YEAR TWO: annual flowers, and the flowers from the tubers and corms I lift annually.
- YEAR THREE: very fine potato production.
- YEAR FOUR: splendid root crops such as beetroot, carrot and parsnips, along with extra-tasty celery and the most aromatic parsley you can imagine.

PREPARATION AND FEEDING: Add layers of vegetable-waste compost, topsoil, old and new straw, manure and leaf mould at the start of the moon's fourth quarter.

THE NATURAL GARDENER

> ### BETTER BY NATURE: TIP #6
> *Let nature have her way*
>
> Don't fight nature when excavating. If, once you've removed the topsoil, you discover compacted industrial deposits, sheer clay or even rock, just accept it and turn it into your shallow-trench bed instead.

How to create your first deep-trench bed (see illustration)

1. Choose one of the four areas in the garden you're committing to the crop-rotation system. Think of this area as your launch area, which will contain your rotation system's first beds: a deep trench, a shallow trench and a single-dug bed.

2. Within your chosen area, choose the site of the deep-trench bed. This is really dictated by the space needed by the most space-consuming crop you'll be planting over the next four years, which, unless you and your whole family are planning on a never-ending zero-carb diet (not recommended), will be: first-early, second-early and main-crop potatoes

3. Plan your bed so there's easy access to the sides for harvesting and management. Remember that in future there will be beds alongside this deep trench. It's going to be 1 metre wide and you'll also need space to heap

John with a basket of heritage apples from Tresillian's orchard. Some varieties date back to the early 1800s. *(©Marianne Majerus 2011)*

Left: Tresillian walled garden in 1986.

Right: Digging the first deep trenches. Hard, hard work but...

Left: ...the results are worth it. First crops are encouraging.

Right: In full flourish: Tresillian's walled kitchen garden today.
(©Marianne Majerus 2011)

Above: The stunning herb garden lies in the centre, attracting bees and deterring pests.

Below: Tresillian House, built in the late eighteenth century, now has estate gardens to match its grandeur.

(©*Marianne Majerus 2011*)

Above: Keep your tool shed in order and it's a pleasant place to take your well-earned rest.

Below: Brassicas thrive when planted, fed and harvested to lunar phases. These winter greens and cabbages grow up to two feet wide.

Above: You need food for the soul, too. Even on the greyest of days, the flowers bordering the garden bring colour and life.

Below: Passing the knowledge on. John's methods have attracted widespread interest from around the world.

Above left: Co-author Jim Rickards, weighing up the advantages of moon gardening.

Above right: Grown under glass, the moon can't take credit for these beauties. But comfrey feed can. *(© Jim Rickards)*

Below: John is famous for his techniques with sweet peas. Some of the varieties he's collected date back to the 1830s. *(© Jim Rickards)*

Above: Moon gardening produces crops like these. Not just super-sized, but super-flavoured, too. *(© Jim Rickards)*

Below: Garlic as big as your fist. A single clove of these garlics is the same size as the standard supermarket garlic bulb. *(© Jim Rickards)*

A freshly picked barrowful, ready for the guests at Tresillian House.
(©Marianne Majerus 2011)

MAKE YOUR BED AND GROW IN IT

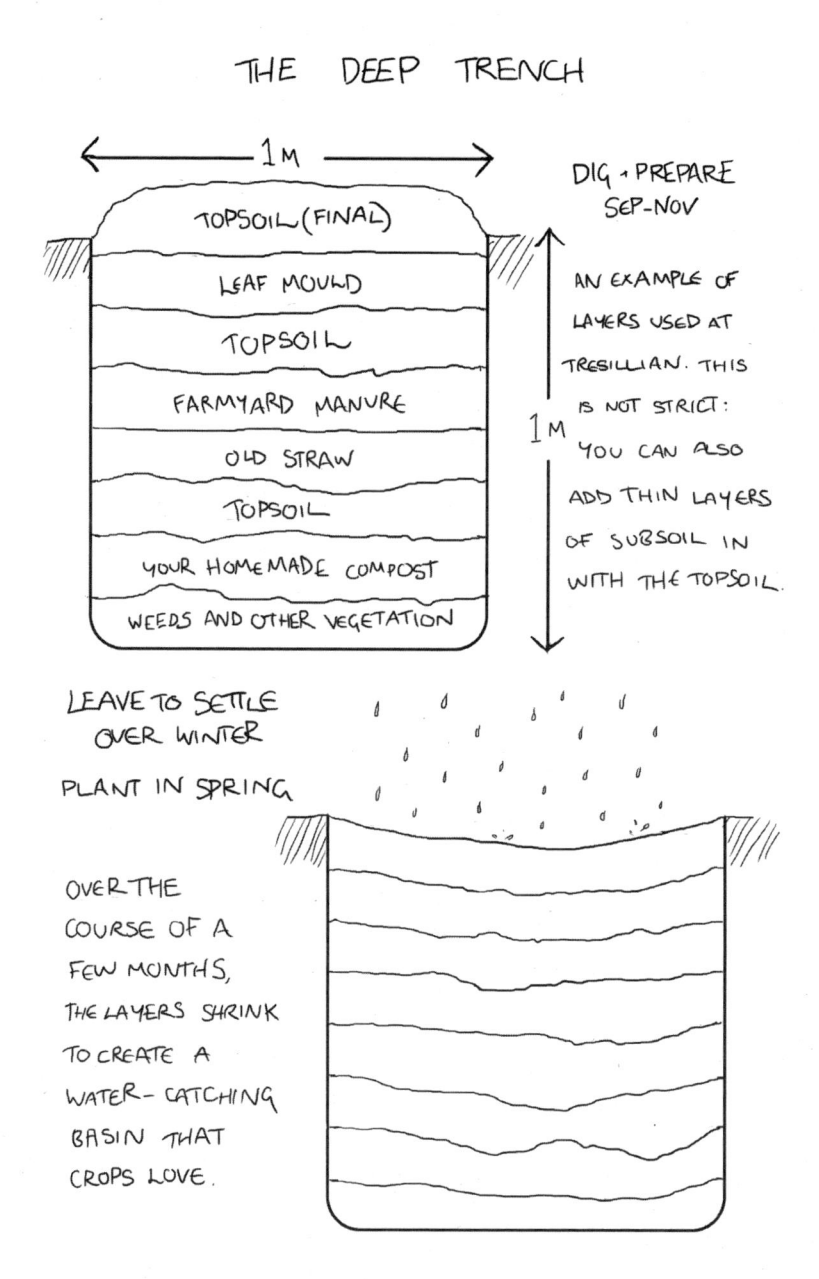

THE DEEP TRENCH

←— 1M —→

TOPSOIL (FINAL)
LEAF MOULD
TOPSOIL
FARMYARD MANURE
OLD STRAW
TOPSOIL
YOUR HOMEMADE COMPOST
WEEDS AND OTHER VEGETATION

1M

DIG + PREPARE SEP-NOV

AN EXAMPLE OF LAYERS USED AT TRESILLIAN. THIS IS NOT STRICT: YOU CAN ALSO ADD THIN LAYERS OF SUBSOIL IN WITH THE TOPSOIL.

LEAVE TO SETTLE OVER WINTER

PLANT IN SPRING

OVER THE COURSE OF A FEW MONTHS, THE LAYERS SHRINK TO CREATE A WATER-CATCHING BASIN THAT CROPS LOVE.

your excavated topsoil and a run for your wheelbarrow to take the heavier subsoil.

4. Before you get going, work out where you're going to put this excavated subsoil. I recommend adding small amounts of the subsoil between your manure and feed layers, because this is the only natural way to turn subsoil into topsoil.

5. At the start of the October moon's third quarter, position two garden lines 1 metre apart, to mark the surface where you're going to dig the trench. The aim is to have the trench fully open no later than the end of the October moon's third quarter, so, if you think it's going to take longer to dig your trench, start a bit earlier.

6. Start removing the topsoil between the lines. First use a fork to loosen up the soil, then get stuck in with your spade to lift and transfer to one side. You're removing the topsoil only temporarily, so it's fine for it to pile up alongside the trench.

7. Topsoil is darker and looser than subsoil. In most gardens it's at least one blade deep. As you remove the topsoil, separate out any turf and annual weeds not in seed. Put these to one side for use in the trench later on.

8. You may come across large stones and hard matter. Separate this out and store for use in some other

project. I take the view that everything that isn't poisonous is a resource to your garden, and have learned from mistakes early on when I completely removed elements from our garden, only to find I of course needed them for something a few seasons later.

9. Once you hit the subsoil, go back to your fork and use it to loosen things up a goodly amount. Then use your spade, or better still a long-handled pointed shovel, to shift the subsoil into your wheelbarrow. It's heavy stuff, so don't overload your barrow.

10. Keep digging the subsoil until the trench is 1 metre wide and 1 metre deep, all the way along its length.

11. Now loosen the bottom of the trench with your fork. Don't skimp at this stage. You don't want a hard pan at the bottom of your deep-trench bed. Natural drainage is vital to keep the roots of your crops healthy and thriving here.

12. You're aiming to be at this stage by the end of the October moon's third quarter at the latest. Achieved that? Good. Now immediately cover the bottom of the trench with the seedless annual weeds and other seedless vegetation you've dug. Then lay any turfs along the bottom, grass side down.

13. Over this, layer a 17–18-centimetre thickness of thoroughly rotted vegetable compost. If this isn't

available, use whatever you've got in your compost bin, regardless of the stage it's reached.

14. Follow the compost layer with the same thickness of the topsoil piled alongside your trench.

15. Follow this with the same thickness of old straw. No old straw? Use fresh. If you have no straw, leave it out but increase the thickness of the other layers. I prefer old straw because it's the stuff animals have lain on and it's lost any traces of farmer's chemicals that may have contaminated it.

16. Add the same thickness of fully composted – at least two-year-old – farmyard manure.

17. Now another layer, same thickness, of your topsoil.

18. Now a layer, same thickness, of at least two-year-composted leaf mould.

19. To finish off, using a sharp garden spade – not a fork – add a final 17–18-centimetre layer of topsoil. This should create a bed surface raised above surrounding ground by about 20 centimetres. Because you've used the spade at this stage, the surface should look like a ploughed field. Flatten and tidy the trench edges with your spade. Ideally, this final layer of topsoil should be finished as the moon moves from third to fourth quarter.

20. The bed is now ready to leave for winter. During this time the raised surface will sink and soon create a rain-collecting depression.

21. Follow the time-honoured method of letting the surface develop weeds through winter. Then, using a spade, uproot them before they set seeds. Compost the annual weeds and their roots; destroy perennial weeds altogether. By doing this, you reduce the potential growth of weeds through the four-year cycle of the trench's life.

22. Come spring, do a final, thorough weeding of the bed surface before you get started on it proper. Use a garden fork to break up the larger clods you first created, then hoe or rake the surface till it's finer and forming a nice tilth.

23. Your deep-trench bed is now ready to start growing the plants you've designated for the first year of your rotation scheme. Follow the moon-gardening timings for feeding and sowing/planting up outlined elsewhere in this book.

24. Over the next three years, complete harvesting by the beginning of the winter and strip the trench of all growth. Deep-dig the surface with a sharp, square-ended spade to restore the wintertime appearance and texture of the ploughed field. Leave like this over winter to let the rains and frosts do their work

and encourage the processes that result in long-term enhanced soil fertility.

25. At the beginning of the fifth winter, the trench is dug out and the layers renewed exactly as before, and the cycle begins all over again.

> ### BETTER BY NATURE: TIP #7
> *Less stooping, more leverage, less effort*
>
> I use a special Cornish shovel for deep-trench work. It has a long, almost straight handle and a pointed blade. The length means you don't stoop so much and it gives you much better leverage. The pointed blade cuts through heaped and loosened earth with much less effort. If you can get hold of one, give it a try. But, in the end, use what you're comfortable with – shovel, spade or fork.

THE SHALLOW-TRENCH BED

SUITABLE FOR: An easier life. You can use the shallow-trench bed instead of the deep-trench version. It's less onerous to dig and quicker to complete. All the plants that like deep trenches will like shallow trenches. As with the deep trench, the powerhouse of the shallow trench is the sponge formed by the bed's layers of topsoil, compost and manure. It's just not as powerful as its deeper brother.

WHAT IT DOES FOR YOUR CROPS: You'll still get good results from it because:

- it provides a rich basis of nutrients; and
- it catches and retains moisture from above via its sunken-bed surface and moisture from below by the moon-raised water table.

WHEN TO DIG IT: Beginning of the September, October or November moon's fourth quarter, preferably September, depending on soil and weather conditions.

DIMENSIONS: 1 metre wide x 50 centimetres deep – length is up to you, based on the size of your garden, how much you want to plant and how much space your chosen crops are going to take up.

WHAT YOU NEED TO DIG IT: Fork, spade, shovel (ideally), two garden lines for guidance and your wheelbarrow to move your excavated subsoil.

CROPS GROWN IN IT VIA ROTATION: The shallow trench should ideally make up one part of one of the four areas of your garden that you designate for four-year crop rotation. Suggested four year cycle:

- YEAR ONE: grow runner beans, climbing French beans, sweet peas, marrows, courgettes and pumpkins.

- YEAR TWO: annual flowers, and the flowers from the tubers and corms I lift annually.
- YEAR THREE: potato production.
- YEAR FOUR: good root crops such as beetroot, carrot and parsnips, with celery and lovely fresh parsley.

PREPARATION AND FEEDING: At the start of the moon's fourth quarter, add layers of vegetable-waste compost, topsoil, old and new straw, manure and leaf mould. Alternatively, layers of compost, topsoil, then a sponge of uncontaminated lawn mowings and shredded fresh leaves.

How to create your first shallow-trench bed

The shallow trench is great, but it won't get the incredible results of the deep trench. It is, however, an excellent way to make best use of smaller gardens and fewer hours in the day.

1. Follow the guidelines outlined for the deep-trench bed but this time the depth is 50 centimetres, not 1 metre. The layers will be 7–8 centimetres thick, not 17–18 centimetres.

2. If you don't have all the vegetable elements for your layers, follow this alternative:

    a. line the bottom of the bed with 10 centimetres of vegetable-waste compost;

    b. follow with 10 centimetres of weeded topsoil,

then 20 centimetres of sponge made from a *either* a compacted layer of weedkiller-free lawn mowings of any age, fresh to blackened, *or* a compacted layer of these lawn mowings mixed in with fresh shredded leaves.

3. After this, fill up the trench with weeded topsoil. Keep adding more topsoil until the bed level is 17–18 centimetres above the surrounding soil.

4. As with the deep trench, leave this unused over winter and plant out/sow in spring.

BETTER BY NATURE: TIP #8
Hey! No hay!

Warning! Do not use hay in place of straw for any of these trenches. Hay's seed content is ripe and of maximum volume (that's why it's so good as an animal feed), but, if you put it into garden soil, it'll generate a lot of grass seed, which will keep plaguing you. And don't be tempted by straw from pet shops either: it's likely to be full of chemicals. Besides, it's very expensive bought this way.

THE SINGLE-DUG BED

SUITABLE FOR: Planting a variety of crops in a single bed in a series of adjacent small trenches. Anything that is not a gross feeder, e.g. carrots, parsnips, white turnips, radishes, lettuce, cabbages, spring onions, kohlrabi. Great for companion planting because they're closer together than deep trenches.

WHAT IT DOES FOR YOUR CROPS: The proper way to manoeuvre and cultivate your soil, well aerated, semi-rough, oxygen gets in and benefits all plants that follow it.

WHEN TO DIG IT: It needs to be completed by the beginning of the September, October or November moon's fourth quarter, preferably September.

DIMENSIONS: As deep and wide as the spade you're using. Length is up to you, based on the size of your garden, how much you want to plant and how much space your chosen crops are going to take up.

WHAT YOU NEED TO DIG IT: Fork, spade, shovel (ideally), four garden lines for guidance and your wheelbarrow to move excess soil and stones etc.

CROPS GROWN IN IT VIA ROTATION: The single-dug trench should ideally make up one part of one of the four areas of your garden that you designate for four-year crop rotation. Suggested four year cycle:

- YEAR ONE: superlative broad beans, broccoli, cabbages, cauliflowers, dwarf French beans, kale, kohlrabi, onions, peas, savoys, spinach, swedes and turnips.

- YEAR TWO: annual flowers, and the flowers from the tubers and corms I lift annually.

- YEAR THREE: potato production. Most potatoes in a deep/shallow trench will perform slightly better than single-dug.

- YEAR FOUR: beetroot, carrots, parsnips, celery and abundant fresh parsley.

PREPARATION AND FEEDING: At the start of the moon's fourth quarter, add composted farm manure to fill the trenches.

How to create your first single-dug bed

1. Single-dug beds can be as many as you like, in parallel. As with the other trenches, this is going to be in Area 1 of your first-year crop rotation, i.e. your launch area. It's going to be dug alongside either deep or shallow trenches, both of which are 1 metre wide, so bear this in mind when planning where to put your beds. Remember, too, that you'll need easy access, preferably to both sides of the beds, so allow for that in your planning.

2. At the start of the September moon's third quarter, mark out the width of your bed (roughly the width of your spade) with two parallel garden lines. The lines will be as long as you want the bed to be. The aim, as with the other trenches, is to complete the bed by the end of the moon's third quarter. This is important

for the single-dug bed because it's the optimum time for adding manure to the ground – because the water table is falling, the ground is most receptive to 'drawing in' added nutrients.

3. Mark out one end of your planned bed with a third garden line. Position this between the ends of the two parallel garden lines. With the fourth garden line, mark out the other end of the planned bed the same way.

4. Dig Trench 1, which will be as long as the width of your entire single-dug bed. Dig inside the garden line, marking out one end of the bed. The depth and width of the trench is simply the size of your spade's blade.

5. Put the topsoil from Trench 1 into a wheelbarrow. Every time it fills up, wheel it over to the other end of your bed area, just beyond your fourth garden line. Don't create a single huge heap of soil, but space each barrowload along the length of the fourth line. This way the earth is ready for use when you reinstate the final trench. Keep digging and filling your wheelbarrow until Trench 1 is finished.

6. As the topsoil is removed, separate out weeds, rubbish and stones as described in previous instructions for the deep trench.

7. As with other trenches, give the bottom of the trench a good going-over with a fork to aid drainage.

MAKE YOUR BED AND GROW IN IT

8. Put the annual seedless weeds and grass-side-down turf at the bottom of the trench.

9. Fill Trench 1 with fully composted (at least two-year-old) farmyard manure.

10. Dig Trench 2 in exactly the same way as Trench 1, positioning it immediately alongside manure-filled Trench 1.

11. Deposit the dug-out topsoil from Trench 2 on top of the manure in Trench 1. Try to be precise here. You want the raised bed to be about 17 centimetres above the level of the surrounding soil.

12. Fill Trench 2 with weeds, turf and manure, as you did Trench 1.

13. Cover Trench 2's manure with the topsoil from digging Trench 3 immediately alongside.

14. Keep doing this until you have as many trenches as you planned for the single-dug bed. On the final trench, you use the topsoil that you barrowed to the end of the bed from Trench 1.

15. The soil surface should be rough, broken, spade-created.

16. Neatly angle the four edges of the raised bed with the flat of your spade.

17. This bed is then sown and planted according to moon-gardening principles in the same way as the other trenches. At the beginning of the fifth winter, the single bed is exhausted, so will need be renewed at the start of the September, October or November moon's third quarter, ready for a new four-year crop rotation cycle.

BETTER BY NATURE: TIP #9
A topping of topsoil

When trench digging, you nearly always end up with excess topsoil. The best way to recycle this is to scatter it as thinly as possible over the widest possible area of your garden beds generally. This keeps the nutrients in the garden but, importantly, hardly increases the thickness of the topsoil above established root systems.

16

pH – The Power of Hydrogen

You've probably read about the pH of soil a hundred times. You can go into the maths and chemistry of it, or you can simply understand the basics and learn what works practically. No prizes for guessing that I've gone for the second option!

The term pH means '*potenz* hydrogen' ('*potenz*' is German for 'power', so literally 'the power of hydrogen'), and for gardening purposes it's an indicator of how acid or alkaline your soil is. It actually measures the level of hydrogen ions in any solution. The more hydrogen there is, the greater the acidity. The scale goes from pH1, meaning extremely acid (you'd find that in the peatiest of peat bogs) to pH14, meaning extremely alkaline (you'd need to go to the beach to find anything approaching that).

The most important one is pH7, which means the soil is absolutely neutral. Water has a pH of 7; most soils are close to

THE NATURAL GARDENER

Plants listed by soil pH preferences (showing the plants' optimum pH ranges)

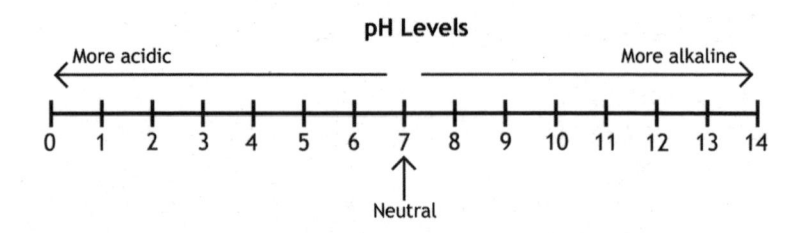

pH Levels

← More acidic   More alkaline →

```
├──┼──┼──┼──┼──┼──┼──┼──┼──┼──┼──┼──┼──┼──┤
0   1   2   3   4   5   6   7   8   9   10  11  12  13  14
                            ↑
                         Neutral
```

Plants for acidic soil ~ pH 4.0 to 5.5

Arbutus (4.0-6.0)
Azalea (4.5-6.0)
Blackberries (5.0-6.0)
Camellias (4.5-5.5)
Erica/heather (4.0-6.0)
Holly (4.5-6.0)
Hydrangeas, blue (4.0-5.0)
Lily of the Valley (4.5-6.0)
Potatoes (4.5-6.0)
Raspberries (5.0-6.5)
Rhododendrons (4.5-6.0)
Rosemary (5.0-6.0)
Spruce (4.0-5.0)

Plants for somewhat acidic soil ~ pH 5.5 to 6.5

Apples (5.0-6.5)
Asparagus (6.0-8.0)
Aubergines (5.5-6.5)
Begonias (5.5-7.0)
Campanulas (5.5-6.5)
Carrots (5.5-7.0)
Clematis (5.5-7.0)
Cucumbers (5.5-7.0)
Gooseberries (5.0-6.5)
Grapes (6.0-7.0)
Jasmine (5.5-7.0)
Lupins (5.5-7.0)
Peanuts (5.0-6.5)
Peppers (5.5-7.0)
Plumbago (5.5-6.5)
Pumpkins (6.0-6.5)
Radicchio (5.5-6.5)
Redcurrants (5.5-7.0)
Rhubarb (5.5-7.0)
Roses, hybrid tea, rambling (5.5-7.0)
Sunflowers (5.0-7.0)
Sweet potatoes (5.5-6.0)
Turnips (5.5-7.0)
Violas (5.5-6.5)

PH – THE POWER OF HYDROGEN

Plants for somewhat acidic soil ~ pH 6.5 to 8.0

Artichokes (6.5-7.5)
Asparagus (6.0-8.0)
Beans French,
 runner, broad (6.0-7.5)
Blackcurrants (6.0-8.0)
Broccoli (6.0-7.0)
Brussels sprouts (6.0-7.5)
Cabbages (6.0-7.5)
Celeriac (6.0-7.0)
Celery (6.0-7.0)
Chives (6.0-7.0)
Cotoneaster (6.0-8.0)
Cyclamens (6.0-7.0)
Delphiniums (6.0-7.5)
Forsythia (6.0-8.0)
Hydrangeas (6.0-7.0)
Kale (6.0-7.5)
Leeks (6.0-8.0)
Lettuce (6.0-7.0)
Mint (7.0-8.0)

Onions (6.0-7.0)
Parsley (5.0-7.0)
Passion flowers (6.0-8.0)
Peaches (6.0-7.5)
Pears (6.0-7.5)
Peas (6.0-7.5)
Peppers (5.5-7.0)
Radishes (6.0-7.0)
Rhubarb (6.5-7.0)
Roses, climbing (6.0-7.0)
Spinach (6.0-7.5)
Squash, summer (6.0-7.0)
Squash, winter (5.5-7.0)
Sunflowers (6.0-7.5)
Swedes (5.5-7.0)
Sweet peas (6.0-7.5)
Turnips (5.5-7.0)
Watercress (6.0-8.0)
Wisteria (6.0-8.0)

Plants with the widest range of pH tolerance ~ between acid pH 5.0 and alkaline pH 7.5 (suitable for most soils)

Asters (5.5-7.5)
Cauliflowers (5.5-7.5)
Fuchsias (5.5-7.5)
Garlic (5.5-7.5)
Maize (5.5-7.5)

Parsnips (5.5-7.5)
Strawberries (5.0-7.5)
Tomatoes (5.5-7.5)
Wallflowers (5.5-7.5)
Zinnias (5.5-7.5)

this level; and most plants will grow fine at this level. So what's the fuss about?

Every plant has a pH preference. The vast majority are between 5 and 7 and will grow OK in your soil whatever you do. But, to get the very best results, the ideal approach is to match the soil pH with your plants' preference. Don't assume the pH level in your garden is consistent. Due to the legacy of previous feeds, fertilisers and the plants growing in it, it may vary from area to area.

HOW DO I WORK OUT THE PH OF MY SOIL?

There are now many standard pH soil-testing kits on the market. They're available in any garden centre and they're simple to use. You just put a soil sample into the test tube provided, add the liquid supplied, shake it up a bit and leave the test tube to stand for a few minutes. Soon the colour of the solution will change. Hold the tube against a colour-match chart to see where the colour fits in the scale, and you have your pH reading.

HOW DO I KNOW WHAT PH MY PLANTS LIKE?

Usually, it's easy to check what they like because there should be a pH number on the seed packet. But, if you don't know, look at the numerous resources online. I've included a table here for the most common food plants and flowers.

PH – THE POWER OF HYDROGEN

WHEN SHOULD I TEST MY SOIL?

When all's said and done, pH identification with the cheap kits is not pinpoint precise. The good news is that most crops and plants will grow in most conditions and produce some sort of a result for you. If you're a spare-time gardener, I can sympathise if you feel life's too short to mind your p's and H's. However, you should test your soil in any of the following situations:

- when you're setting up your moon garden for planting fruit and/or veg for the first time – if the pH varies you can design your garden to suit;
- when growth seems to be disappointing, no matter what you do;
- when the leaves of your plants are yellowing;
- when you need to maximise output from your patch, e.g. you're feeding your family year-round from your allotment; and
- when you're a perfectionist.

BALANCING YOUR SOIL AFTER THE TEST

The best time to do any soil rebalancing is in the autumn, when the ground is cool, preferably digging in the moon's last quarter.

Here's a quick list of what the results mean, and what to do about them:

pH BELOW 5.0: You have an extremely acid soil. At this level, many essential plant nutrients, especially nitrogen, calcium, copper, magnesium and potassium, are easily depleted from the soil because they dissolve and get washed away by the elements. Phosphates become locked in, so that plants can't feed off them. Bacteria can't rot compost, so your plants can't get any nutrients from them. (This is why perfectly preserved human bodies from thousands of years ago have been found in peat bogs.)

HOW TO FIX IT: Add lime until the pH is at least above 5. In most cases it'll need to be higher.

pH 5.0–6.0: This is an acid soil, which is great for lime-hating plants (known as ericaceous) such as camellias, azaleas, rhododendrons, blueberries and many varieties of potato.

HOW TO FIX IT: The ideal scenario is to put plants in that love this type of soil. However, if all your soil's like this, no matter how big your family, you can't just feed them potatoes and blueberries, let alone rhododendrons. So, as before, add lime to take it closer to the standard soil balance of 6.5–7.0 pH.

pH 6.0–7.0: This is a mildly acidic to neutral soil that most plants will relish . At 7.0 it is neither alkaline nor acid. Bacteria, animals, insects, worms and most plants love this soil. Nutrients are easily accessed and remain in the soil longer.

PH – THE POWER OF HYDROGEN

How to fix it: There's nothing to fix. Congratulations!

pH 7.0–8.0 or higher: This is an alkaline soil, often accompanied by poor soil structure. It is very high in salts and, as the soil gets more alkaline, many plants find it increasingly difficult to absorb nutrients. Some plants love alkaline soil, such as olives and pomegranates, but you're unlikely to be growing these in the UK.

How to fix it: Balancing this type of soil naturally can be a slow job, taking two or three winters, but it is worth it. Use any decomposed compost that doesn't contain grass cuttings. The ideal is for it to have almost gone black, like peat.

17

Friends and Enemies – the Secrets of Compatible Planting

After over fifty years of experimenting in my gardens big and small, there is not a shred of doubt in my mind that some plants help or harm each other when planted side by side. As in all aspects of nature, there are friends and enemies, and it's no different in the plant world. As you keep hearing me saying, everything is variable and everything is connected, so to get the best results from your moon garden follow some of these simple rules and it'll make the difference between good results and exceptional results. We see it season after season at Tresillian, so it should work for you, too.

Note that, in the 'Keep these apart' list, you can deliberately do so if you want to exploit natural weed control.

THE NATURAL GARDENER

Plant these together

- all beans with asparagus, borage, buckwheat, cabbage family, carrots, cauliflowers, celery, cucumbers, leeks, peas, poached-egg flowers, potatoes, squashes, strawberries, sweetcorn, sweat peas, turnips
- all herbs with the cabbage family
- all peas with all beans, carrots, celery, cucumbers, leeks, radishes, swedes, sweetcorn, turnips
- asparagus with all beans, parsley, tomatoes
- basil with tomatoes
- beetroots with kohlrabi
- borage with all beans
- buckwheat with all beans
- cabbage family with all beans, all herbs, cucumbers, marigolds, potatoes
- carrots with all beans, chives, garlic, leeks, lettuce, marigolds, onions, parsley, peas, sage, turnips
- cauliflowers with all beans
- celery with all beans, dill, leeks, all peas, potatoes
- chives with carrots, cucumbers
- cucumbers with all beans, the cabbage family, chives, peas, potatoes
- dill with celery
- garlic with carrots
- horseradish with potatoes
- kohlrabi with beetroots, onions
- leeks with all beans, carrots, celery, lettuce, peas, turnips
- lettuce with carrots, leeks, radishes, strawberries, sweetcorn
- marigolds (calendula) with the cabbage family, carrots
- marigolds (Mexican) with potatoes
- mint with the cabbage family
- onions with carrots, kohlrabi
- parsley with asparagus, carrots, tomatoes
- poached-egg flowers with all beans
- potatoes with all beans, the cabbage family, celery, cucumbers, horseradish, Mexican marigolds, peas, radishes, strawberries, sweetcorn
- pumpkins with sweetcorn
- radishes with lettuce, peas

FRIENDS AND ENEMIES – THE SECRETS OF COMPATIBLE PLANTING

- sage with carrots
- squashes with all beans
- strawberries with all beans, lettuce, potatoes
- swedes with peas
- sweetcorn with all beans, lettuce, peas, potatoes, pumpkins
- sweet peas with all beans
- tomatoes with asparagus, basil, parsley
- turnips with all beans, carrots, leeks, peas

Keep these apart

- all beans and beetroots, garlic, kohlrabi, onions
- all peas and garlic, onions, shallots
- asparagus and garlic, onions
- beetroots and all beans
- cabbage family and garlic, onions, rue, strawberries, vines
- camomile and potatoes
- couch grass and lupins, tomatoes, turnips
- garlic and all beans, asparagus, the cabbage family, all peas, strawberries
- ground elder and Mexican marigolds
- ground ivy and Mexican marigolds
- kohlrabi and all beans, tomatoes
- lupins and couch grass
- Mexican marigolds and ground elder, ground ivy
- mint and potatoes
- olive tree and oak tree
- onions and all beans, asparagus, the cabbage family, peas, strawberries
- potatoes and camomile, mint, pumpkins, rosemary, sunflowers, thyme, tomatoes
- pumpkins and potatoes
- rosemary and potatoes
- rue and the cabbage family
- shallots and all peas
- strawberries and the cabbage family, garlic, onions
- sunflowers and potatoes
- thyme and potatoes
- tomatoes and couch grass, kohlrabi, potatoes
- turnips and couch grass
- vines and the cabbage family

BETTER BY NATURE: TIP #10

Not welcome here!

If you plant lots of mixed aromatic herbs around your vegetable beds, it confuses and discourages unwelcome pest insects. It's also a lovely colourful addition to your hardworking kitchen garden.

BETTER BY NATURE: TIP #11
In good company

When planting peas and beans, always remember that certain crops do well in their company. Lettuces and radishes, the staple diet of many a salad plate, are best grown in the company of peas and beans because they do not like direct sunshine, doing better with filtered light. The trellises and wigwams of the climbers break the light over your lettuces, protecting from harsh direct heat. They also benefit from the root system of peas and beans, which generates its own nitrogen. Lettuces, radishes and similar are fast-growing and thrive off the residue of the nitrogen release of peas and beans. This is but one of many examples of compatible planting that have often been forgotten because superficially fast

FRIENDS AND ENEMIES – THE SECRETS OF COMPATIBLE PLANTING

good results can always be achieved by adding fertilisers. (Modern commercial growers contracted to supply the big supermarkets with thousands of salad products every day cannot use this method, as they have to resort to modern varieties, modern spraying and modern irrigation and highly chemical feeding. This is the price the nation pays to get food from the supermarkets on a daily basis, regardless of the season. But you don't have to.)

18

Fertilisers, Manures and Feeds

In our walled Victorian kitchen garden and across the Tresillian estate, I use several different fertilisers, animal manures, potash, vegetable manures and the best one of all, comfrey stock, along with nettle tea. They're all organic, and the trick is always to apply them specifically, area by area, in controlled quantities.

There's one golden rule I always follow with fertiliser: it can be 'man-produced' and 'man-managed' but never 'man-made'. The animal and vegetable manures are more than solely feeds, so they require a different approach.

I use these organic fertilisers . . .

- fish, blood and bone – this is a good general fertiliser sterilised bonemeal

- dolomite limestone
- gypsum
- hoof and horn
- calcified seaweed
- seaweed meal

. . . and these manures

- farmyard manure – a mixture of the product of all farm creatures except horses
- stable manure – solely from horses
- vegetable manure – rotted vegetable waste from our kitchen (never use meat, however, not even scrapings from plates or pans, as it will attract vermin such as rats and foxes)

FERTILISERS

Which fertiliser to use, where?

Product	Main plant foods	Use	Which plants love it?
Rock phosphate	Phosphorus	Correction of phosphorus deficiency, slow-acting	All plants, but flowers, tree root systems, lawns and strawberries in particular

FERTILISERS, MANURES AND FEEDS

Dolomite	Calcium, magnesium	To correct calcium or magnesium deficiency	All plants that prefer a balanced soil
Rock potash	Potassium, trace elements	Adds potassium, but released very slowly	Great for gooseberries and cooking apples
Gypsum	Calcium, sulphur	Corrects sulphur or calcium deficiency, good general soil reconditioner	All plants benefit from improved soil conditions
Bonemeal	Phosphorus, nitrogen, calcium	For long-term plantings, especially when phosphorus levels are low, slow-acting	Apples, flowers and flowering shrubs, developing fruit, lawns, and for when you want to encourage root growth in carrots, parsnips, turnips etc.
Boneflour	Phosphorus, nitrogen, calcium	Quicker-acting source of the same.	As above
Hoof and horn	Nitrogen	Great nitrogen source for poor soils, releases over a long period	Particularly good for green veg, leafy plants and high feeders such as tomatoes.
Seaweed meal	Nitrogen, potassium	Useful source of potassium. Quicker acting.	General feed and soil improver, great for improving lawns

Calcified seaweed	Calcium, magnesium and trace elements	As a soil conditioner and to raise the pH	Apricots, cabbage family, all green vegetables, lawns, nectarines, peaches and plums
Fish, blood and bone	Phosphorus, nitrogen	A good general fertiliser, quick-acting.	Broad-leafed plants, cabbage family, courgettes, cucumbers, flowers, grapes, green vegetables, lawns, lettuces, marrows, peas, potatoes, pumpkins, fast-growing plants, runner beans and all salad crops generally

Fish, blood and bone

This fertiliser is high in fast-acting nitrogen, but has no phosphates. It encourages strong root systems and is superb for general-purpose use. Application: 60–80 grams per square metre of bed surface for general use, salad crops and earthing up potatoes; 115 grams per square metre for the hungry ones – such as potatoes, cabbages and brassicas generally.

Sterilised bonemeal

This gives your garden slow-release organic phosphates. It promotes strong root growth over a long period of time. Application: 115–145 grams per square metre when planting new shrubs and trees.

Dolomite limestone

You'll only need to use this if your soil is too acidic for the plants you want to grow and you don't want to put it anywhere near your lime-hating plants such as rhododendrons. So, first thing is to test your soil using a pH testing kit – see Page 128. Application: generally, 200–250 grams per square metre, depending on the results of your test.

Gypsum

This is a godsend if you've got a heavy clay soil. It improves the aeration and drainage, thus promoting healthier, happier plants. Application: 250–500 grams per square metre.

Hoof and horn

This is a completely natural, slow-acting source of organic nitrogen. Great for most green vegetables and lawns that need their colour strengthened. Application: 75–130 grams per square metre.

Calcified seaweed

This is amazing stuff. Along with calcium, it contains magnesium and many other trace elements that are wonderful for general soil conditioning. But it really comes into its own for encouraging stone fruits, such as plums. (By the way, an old Edwardian trick was to grow fruit trees on builders' rubble for the lime in the mortar. Today, cement mortar doesn't contain the lime the trees need, so don't try it in your garden.) Calcified seaweed sweetens the soil and creates a better stone. The better the stone, the better the fruit. Application: for fruit trees, apply in January 115–175 grams per square metre directly onto the soil surface around the base of the tree. For feeding cabbages and other brassicas add 60–80 grams per square metre.

Seaweed meal

A slow-acting, long-lasting plant food, this meal is rich in trace elements and aids soil improvement. Application: 60–120 grams per square metre as a lawn feed, promoting strong growth and rich colour. The same level is also excellent as a general soil feed. Lightly rake it in three months before you plant. Come planting time, the soil's bacteria will have broken it down beautifully.

Rotted vegetable waste

Everyone has vegetable waste from their garden and their kitchen (we have heaps of the stuff at Tresillian) and it is a waste not to use it for compost. But the system we use at Tresillian is fairly elaborate and probably overkill for most gardens and allotments. (If you'd like full details of our system, please see my *Moon Gardening*, published in 2002 by Really Useful Books.)

So, for your average garden, allotment or even a small urban garden, you need two containers to put your compost in. You can safely add all vegetable kitchen waste plus garden cuttings,

FERTILISERS, MANURES AND FEEDS

leaves and the occasional egg box for texture. Try to avoid adding cooked food or meat because this attracts vermin, though some gardeners do swear by adding these for an extra-rich compost. I personally feel it's not worth the potential bother of attracting foxes or rats, but it is up to you. You can, essentially, put pretty much all kitchen waste into your compost heap.

The reason you should go for two bins is to keep the compost moving and aerated. Every six weeks or so, shift the compost from one bin to the other, turning it and mixing as you do so. The more you activate it, the greater the bacterial activity, the quicker it all breaks down into usable compost. Leave it alone and you run the risk of turning it into a great big sticky mess, which could go stagnant and turn rancid.

You can either use black bins with lids or build wood-sided compost pits. Practically speaking, bins with a trapdoor at the bottom, like an old-fashioned coal bunker, are ideal because they allow easy access to the fully rotted compost at the bottom.

The three golden rules of composting

1. LITTLE AND OFTEN. Try not to put too much in, in one go. Have a baby compost bin in your kitchen and, as soon as it's nearly full, take it out to your garden and add it. Don't keep cramming more stuff into your kitchen compost bin until it's a solid, stubborn mass that refuses to budge even if you tip it upside down. By mixing in little bits every day, you also keep it moving almost without thinking.

2. Keep water content down. If you want to add tealeaves, for instance (gardens love tealeaves and coffee grounds), strain them first. Too much moisture makes for stinky compost bins.

3. Go for variety and bulk. The more varied the vegetable waste, the better your compost. Too much of one thing could give you a 'lopsided' compost with an excess of one nutrient. Bulking compost with straw or the occasional shredded egg box helps to absorb moisture and helps with aeration.

My secret compost cheat

I have a friend who makes the most amazing tea. And, when I asked him how he does it, he said mysteriously, 'It's all in the blend.' But I watched him one day and he uses a mix of loose-leaf tea, Turkish full-leaf tea and Yorkshire teabags. So there's a bit of the purist in the mix (Turkish), some good-old fashioned tea (loose-leaf) and good, strong commercial stuff (Yorkshire). All of these teas alone are very nice. Together, they're incredible. So, my cheat is to mix my homemade compost half and half with John Innes composts 1, 2 and 3. All these varieties of John Innes composts are peat-free, organic and recycled and they provide the perfect balance for all the jobs I need doing in the garden, from potting to planting out. (You'll find details of John Innes composts later.)

FERTILISERS, MANURES AND FEEDS

> **BETTER BY NATURE: TIP #12**
> *Caring for your fertiliser naturally*
>
> As soon as I get a delivery of fertiliser I empty it immediately into storage boxes made of wood, which keeps it dry. Each box has a tight-fitting lid, marked by name. At Tresillian, it's stored in the potting shed, but you just need to find a cool dry place. The problem with leaving fertiliser in plastic is that it can quickly deteriorate through sweating or contamination if the bag gets punctured.

Potash

As its name suggests, this fertiliser is high in potassium. It's a critical addition to your garden with ingredients that improve crop yields, help resistance to diseases and increase water retention. It also improves food taste and texture. And roses in particular love it. You have an endless supply of potash, free and natural, from your garden bonfire, as long as you're strict about putting only wood on it – anything from bush prunings to tree and hedgerow cuttings. The ash left over from the fire must be dry-stored the moment it is cold. Any atmospheric moisture or rain will render it useless.

If you have a working fireplace in your home, a great way to ensure good potash is to save all your garden wood for Christmas and enjoy a good open fire for a day or two using only wood. Application: unknown. The best rates can't be determined because the potash element varies with the type and age of the wood you burn. You can't go wrong if you apply it liberally, but don't go too thick or it will cake if it rains.

MANURES

The more fertile your topsoil, the better your plants will flourish. Old-fashioned manure is the best thing to increase the fertility of your topsoil, because it opens up the soil structure. It does this in two ways:

1. it adds bulk, especially when the manure is mixed with straw; and
2. because it feeds the soil it attracts more of the worms and insects you want to keep the soil healthy.

I can't emphasise enough how important it is to naturally encourage the worms and insects of the soil into your garden. They create an aerating structure by tunnelling and forming passageways. The more there are, the more tunnels, passageways and openness – all of which admit air.

For the moon gardener, this is vital, because we depend on the natural rise and fall of the water table, so we need soil conditions to be perfect to make the most of this. Air draws in warmth and moisture, and the manure retains the moisture. Air, manure, warmth and moisture combine to encourage bacteria to thrive in the soil. The bacteria decompose vegetable and animal matter, which along with the warm aerated soil, creates the environment plants need to grow from seed to full maturity.

FERTILISERS, MANURES AND FEEDS

And don't forget the nutrients produced by the worms and insects as they ingest, digest and excrete their fellow creatures, supporting the entire complicated, virtuous biological cycle of life.

Good, balanced topsoil is a thing to be treasured. It takes some time to attain, and it's easy to ruin. Soil is mankind's main food provider, and needs to be protected from uninformed 'additions'.

The best manure of all . . .

. . . is your garden spade or fork. Not enough gardeners really appreciate this. Professional horticulturalists have known it for years, though. The word 'manuring' comes from the word 'manoeuvring', referring to the timeless technique of digging, lifting, turning and replacing the soil back in its broken form. The word 'manoeuvring' came from the ancient French '*maynoverer*', which itself derived from the Latin '*manu operari*' – to work by hand. Which just goes to show that turning the soil by hand, like so much in horticulture, goes back to ancient times and is still with us as an unchanged technique.

Manoeuvring or deep digging – or even 'bastard digging' as it was once aptly known – is by far the best way to get essential air, warmth and moisture into the soil to encourage the vital bacteria that will break down organic matter, both animal and vegetable.

Digging the waning moon

Digging works throughout the moon month, but is especially effective during the third and fourth quarters of the lunar cycle. This is when the water table is sinking and the topsoil is much readier to draw in whatever you apply to it, including air, warmth and moisture. The best thing about this is that manoeuvring increases soil fertility even without adding any kind of plant food. The only cost is the time put in – but it's a great way to keep healthy!

The reason it works so well is that nature abhors a vacuum. The very best time to feed is at the beginning of the third quarter. The soil has been moistened by the previous fortnight of a rising water table and you are adding feed just as the water table is about to fall, so you get the full two weeks of drawing-in working on your feed application.

Bag it before you bin it

If you're getting manure from a farmer or other supplier, make sure you ask for it tied up in sacks. That way, you avoid shovelling and wheelbarrowing loose, stinking manure about your garden. So listen hard when your supplier says blithely, 'I'll drop you off a load.' Stop him right there, because 'drop off a load' means exactly that. In my early days, I've had a lorry load of loose, wet manure tipped at the front gates. It's not a thing to be welcomed, and it didn't happen again.

My manure bins are wooden, a generous cubic metre in size, and, most importantly, they have no bottom. Whatever

FERTILISERS, MANURES AND FEEDS

you put in it rests directly on the soil, which is a must. If you can't get hold of, or build, a wooden container, you can use a black-plastic, bottomless, lidded vegetable-waste composter. These have superb moisture and heat retention and contain the smells well.

Park your sacks of manure by the bins, empty them into your containers. Mix the manure with as much general waste vegetable matter as you have available. I also add loosened bale straw until I get a nice strawy mix. You're adding at this time because the first day of the moon's first quarter heralds the fortnight during which the least loss of moisture into the earth from stored manure can be expected, because the water table is rising and exerting upward, repelling pressure. This timing is important, because maximum moisture is essential for encouraging bacteria and insect life and composting your manure. You want to get it off to a good start.

To keep odours down, cover the surface of the manure with a combination of any and/or all of the following: 8–10 centimetres of leaf mould, topsoil, peat, upside-down common turf, lawn mowings, weighted-down straw or gravel. Make sure any additions haven't been treated with weedkillers of any kind.

I leave my manure containered for at least one year, normally two. Ideally, you should do the same, but I understand the time pressures of today's lifestyle, so, if you're a part-time gardener, don't feel too guilty if you use it sooner. Just remember, the longer you leave it, the more time you give bacteria to feed on the vegetable matter present, encouraging decay and increasing the nutrients when you apply it to your topsoil.

Once a month, again at the start of the moon's first quarter, try to remove the capping and put it in another container. This adds air and warmth to the manure.

> ### BETTER BY NATURE: TIP #13
> *Know what manure you're buying*
>
> STABLE MANURE: Never buy the stuff with wood shavings in it. This is bad for the soil. It must be straw-based. You also need to the straw in a decomposed state.
>
> PIG MANURE: Avoid this. It almost always contains toxins, which got into the feed given by the farmer. You don't want these anywhere near where you're growing food.
>
> COMMERCIALLY BAGGED MANURE: If time is short, there's nothing wrong with going down this road. But avoid the popular dried stuff, which is poultry-based and more of a feed than a conditioner. Get the bagged stuff from your local garden centre, which is composted horse or farmyard manure. It's ready to use, is consistently of a good standard and convenient to handle and store. But it isn't cheap.

FERTILISERS, MANURES AND FEEDS

> ## BETTER BY NATURE: TIP #14
> *Follow the golden triangle*
>
> Old-time gardeners remembered which plants to feed with which fertilisers by following the three points of golden triangle:
>
> - nitrogen for leaf growth;
> - phosphate for robust roots; and
> - potash for plentiful flowers and fruit.

FEEDS

The magic of comfrey

There isn't space in this book to explore the many uses and qualities of comfrey, except to say it has been prized by cultures across Europe and Asia for 2,500 years for many applications, including poultices, treatments of maladies and cuts, drunk as tea and even the healing of bones.

For the moon gardener, it is a natural, organic nitrogen- and potash-rich feed when turned into a solution. Plants flourish under it, it costs nothing to produce and, once set up, the plant is easy to grow and offers you an unlimited supply.

Bees adore comfrey. Its misty-blue blossom draws them into the garden and then gets them pollinating all your other plants. (We're lucky enough on the Tresillian Estate to have two beehives

Magical comfrey

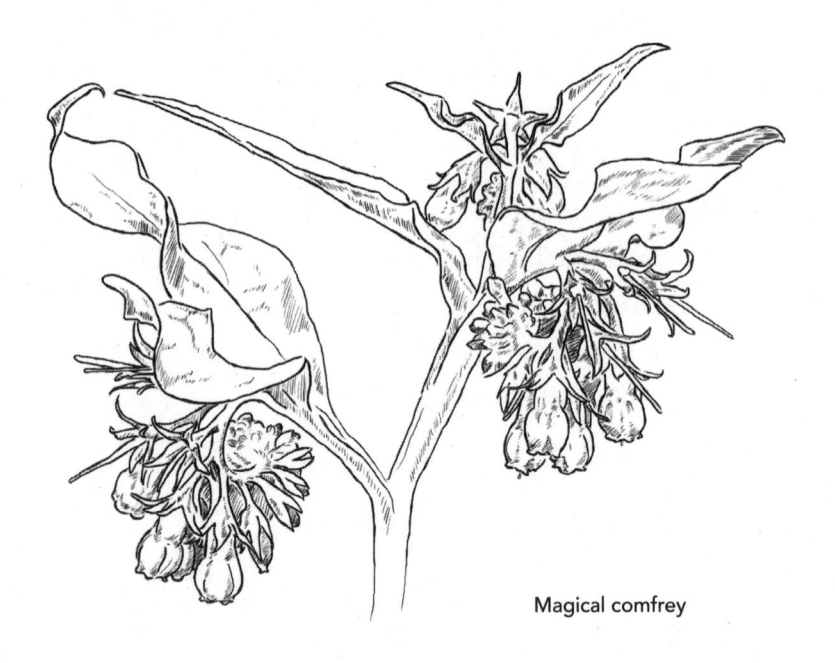

and their busy workers in our walled garden, which have been with us for as long as I can remember. Along with them are the many wild bees that live in the beech trees elsewhere on the estate. All are attracted to the comfrey and help our plants flourish there.)

A word of caution, though. Comfrey is its own master, one of nature's great survivors. It establishes itself, develops, thrives and multiplies with no help from anyone else. Indeed, once it has arrived in your garden and decided it likes where it is, it will stay – no matter what you do with it. Only the removal from the soil of every last scrap of its roots will stop it.

So, to get the best from it, and to keep it contained, plant it, if you can, in what I like to call 'marginal land'. Ideally, this is on the fringes of water, but, since the vast majority of gardeners

FERTILISERS, MANURES AND FEEDS

don't have a stream running through their back garden, I've put together a step-by-step for you . . .

How to grow comfrey, step by step

Comfrey isn't fussy. It will grow in just about any conditions, but if you have a semi-wild bit of your garden, especially if it's damp, it'll be perfect there. However, you need to keep it contained, and away from your herb garden, because, left to itself, it will smother everything in its vicinity. For optimum harvests, follow the steps below, but if you're busy just plant it and keep an eye on it.

1. Buy one or two potted comfrey plantlets. Any time is fine, but buying them earlier in the year gives them more growing time before they face their first winter in the ground.

2. At the start of the moon's second quarter, just before you plant out the comfrey, stand the pots in water for at least two hours, towards the end of the day. (This is good practice for all plants going from pot to garden. The plant has the whole cool night ahead to help it recover from the trauma of transplantation. Evaporation is low, the chosen moon time ensures the moisture of the ground is high, combining to form ideal conditions for planting out.)

3. You have two main choices about where to plant:

   a. NATURAL: Dot the plantlets haphazardly around your garden in unusable corners where they won't compete with your other plants.

   b. REGIMENTED: In a single row, 45 centimetres apart in a 45-centimetre-wide bed. You should establish the bed in margin land, for instance at the foot of your fence that divides your garden from your neighbour's. The only consideration is that the comfrey will need sufficient sunlight and not be too sheltered from rainfall.

4. Whichever approach you choose, go for damp ground, sunlit for most of the day. If that's not available, plant it where you can water it easily. Comfrey's 95 per cent water and it will thank you. You could also lay a seep hose through the patch and set it for one or two hours overnight. This will create the constantly damp conditions in which it thrives, without troubling you too much.

5. You don't need to prepare the ground, just get rid of weeds and loosen with a fork.

6. With a trowel, dig holes the same size as your pots. Put plant with pot in the hole and adjust the depth so that the rim is level with the surrounding ground, then firm the earth around the pot. Pull the pot out, remove the plantlet from the pot. Loosen the earth at the base

FERTILISERS, MANURES AND FEEDS

of the hole using a hand fork for good drainage. Even though comfrey loves water, you don't want its roots to rot.

7. To remove from the pot to promote maximum growth, place the pot upright in the palm of one hand. Spread the fingers of your other hand over the top of the pot around the stem. Grip the top of the pot with the tips of your spread fingers and gently turn it upside down. With fingers still spread, support the compost and slide the plant out slowly. You may need to tap the base of the pot a little. Hold the compost root ball still upside down in the palm of your hand, then cup with the other hand to turn it upright gently. You want to avoid compressing the roots. Now slip the plant into the hollow. It should fit perfectly. Firm the compost around the root ball, depressing its surface a little below the ground. This creates a rain collecting depression.

8. Once it's planted out, water immediately and thoroughly, using a can with a medium rose.

9. Don't harvest for the first two years of the plants' lives. Comfrey needs to establish its root systems without above-ground loss. Pluck off blossom, however, to encourage development.

10. At the end of Year 1 and Year 2, let the top growth die down and return to the soil.

11. In Year 3, you can start harvesting for your first-ever stock making! Cut right back to the ground with shears.

12. After this, you can harvest annually, as soon as the leaves and stems are developed enough for stock, the compost bin or for laying your trench bed, if you're using them.

13. To speed up leaf and stem growth, feed with liquid manure at the beginning of the season. Repeat monthly at the start of the moon's fourth quarter. Before applying any liquid manure, water the plants well and always try to pre-water and feed in the cool of the end of the day.

14. To make the liquid manure, mix a cup or two of proprietary dried manure into a garden bucketful of water. Let the mixture rest for a couple of hours before use. (This ensures the manure absorbs completely in the water.) Comfrey prefers poultry-based manure. A good source is 6X Fertiliser, which may be found online if your local garden suppliers don't stock it.

15. Comfreys are cannibals, so, once they're up and running, you can feed them comfrey solution. Every time you water, dilute one part comfrey stock with eighty parts water. If you're using a seep hose, add comfrey at a 1:40 ratio at the start of the moon's fourth quarter.

FERTILISERS, MANURES AND FEEDS

16. In October of Year 3, and every October afterwards, cut plants down to ground level and transfer the leaves and stems to your compost bin/heap or one of your trenches, if you are using them.

17. Weed immediately after the cut back, recycling in your compost or destroying completely.

BETTER BY NATURE: TIP #15
Tomatoes love comfrey

Comfrey stock is cheaper and better than any tomato feed you can buy in the shops – and it's completely organic.

For tomatoes under glass, artificial conditions or in pots, apply one part comfrey, one part nettle to ten parts water. But when you start feeding, start quarter-strength, then half-strength up to full-strength, when the tomatoes are in full production. For tomatoes only, always water and feed in the morning, not at night. This helps to eliminate blight, which is caused by damp and cold.

For tomatoes in open ground, feed during the last quarter and in the evening, so that the moisture of the liquid feed is not affected by the sun and evaporation. Obviously, you can feed your plants at other times during the month if you need to, especially if they're failing or looking a bit ropey. You should be able to tell, because hungry plants become stunted and will set seed rather than develop a root structure, so it can reproduce before dying.

WARNING! The underside of comfrey leaves is as rough as sandpaper. Wear good gloves when handling and grow it where bare legs won't brush against it, especially if children play in your garden.

Making comfrey stock, step by step

1. Start harvesting the stems and leaves at the beginning of the moon's third quarter (around full moon). This is when the plant is most charged with sap, because the water table is at its highest and the at soil its moistest.

2. Cut the comfrey at ground level with shears. Be careful not to pull off or break the stems. You're looking for a tidy, clean cut.

3. Shred the leaves and stems or cut them into small pieces. An easy way to do this is throw everything into a garden bucket and attack them with very sharp hedge shears. You soon have perfectly milled comfrey matter ready to go in the stock.

4. Put 1 kilogram of shredded comfrey into 11 litres of cold rain or tap water in a nonmetallic container. The cheap 80-litre plastic dustbins with lids are ideal.

FERTILISERS, MANURES AND FEEDS

5. Keep adding 1 kilogram comfrey to 11 litres of water until you've filled the container or run out of comfrey.

6. Replace the lid to keep out the light (and stop any animals falling in and drowning), and date the container so you'll know how long your brew's been steeping.

7. Leave to brew for at least one calendar month, giving it a good stir every now and then.

8. After one month, your stock is ready to turn into solution. For a standard solution mix one part filtered stock to eighty parts cold water. The stock doesn't deteriorate if you keep it in the plastic container.

9. It's always a good idea to end the growing season with a fully charged container full of comfrey stock, so you're ready to start feeding your plants come the next spring, because your comfrey plants won't be ready for harvest until about June.

> **BETTER BY NATURE: TIP #16**
> *Stocking up*
>
> The best comfrey stock brewer is a plastic rainwater butt raised high enough off the ground to enable you to put a bucket underneath the tap. Draw off stock, whenever you need it. You may need to fit a gauze filter inside the butt to stop the leaves and stems blocking the tap. To avoid annoying blockages, you may need to filter the stock again before using it in your watering can or seep hose.

Feeding and watering with comfrey

GENERAL WATERING WITH COMFREY: This is not moon-oriented, so do this whenever you normally water your plants. In the cool of an evening, apply a 1:80 solution in a watering can with rose directly onto the plant leaves, or the soil at the base of the plant stems, as a general moisturiser.

FEEDING WITH COMFREY: Feeding *is* moon-oriented, so you should do this at the start of the moon's fourth quarter at a solution ratio of 1:40.

Using nettle or dandelion feeds

Comfrey, nettle and dandelion are all compatible with each other, both when growing side by side and when feeding your

FERTILISERS, MANURES AND FEEDS

plants. They all contain complementary yet different trace elements at different levels. Trace elements in the soil are like vitamins to us. Where we would get rickets without Vitamin D, soil after too much rain can be leached of nutrients such as magnesium and calcium, and stunt the growth of whatever is growing there. This particularly applies to soil that's been uncared for and compacted down. It goes green with moss and algae and can't breathe.

Nettle tea

Nettles are rich in many of the nutrients your plants crave: nitrogen, phosphorous, calcium, copper and iron. The best way to get it into your garden and working hard for you is to make tea with it. Be warned: it does stink – so don't think it's gone off when you get hit by that smell!

To make the tea:

1. Stuff a bucket or barrel full of nettles.

2. Cover with water. Rainwater is best, because it has no added chemicals, but tap water is fine.

3. Leave to steep and stew for about a month and not longer than five weeks.

4. Hold your nose and strain.

5. You can pour a little of the strained liquid direct onto your compost heap.

6. With the rest, you can fertilise growing plants by diluting one part nettle tea to at least ten parts water.

Dandelion tea

Like their friend, comfrey, dandelions have deep roots constantly searching for the earth's nutrients, so they make an excellent feed. Follow the same steps as for nettle tea, though you may find you'll have enough for only smaller batches. Don't use the seed heads in the brew, because you don't want them all over your garden!

19

Stand Your Ground

A little point to make at the end of Part Two of this book: you will get raised eyebrows, and you may get people scoffing at you if you say you garden by the phases of the moon. I've had this all my life and it's fine. I'm the loony gardener. But I'm also the one with award-winning produce, huge crop yields and extra-tasty veg on my plate every night.

It's easy to dismiss something that doesn't fit in with the mass view of how things should be done. Understandably, people are sceptical – the science is ambiguous and people argue that it hasn't been repeatable under strict conditions. There is also a lot of misunderstanding because other versions of Moon Gardening are much more deeply rooted in astrology and star signs, something that I, personally, am not proposing.

I've researched and tested the techniques illustrated here and I know absolutely that the moon affects how plants grow, because I see it every day on Tresillian Estate. I think the rational explanation is down to the increase and decrease in moisture in the soil, caused by a rising and falling water table. But there may well be other factors at play – increased insect and animal activity, or fluctuating nocturnal light, for instance. Gardening is all about controlling the variables to your advantage: testing, testing and testing again, then repeating and fine-tuning what works for you in your patch.

So stand your ground and tell people to try it properly first before coming to any conclusion. Or give them a bunch of the sweetest, juiciest carrots they've ever tasted. Sometimes, that's all the proof you need.

Combining traditional, natural methods of feeding with-moon phase planting and harvesting can lead to spectacular results.

Part Three

The Proof is in the Planting . . .

. . . and the pruning, and the trading, and the fishing

20

When We Stopped Moving, We Started Growing

Ever since mankind first decided it might be easier to stick around and build fences rather than keep chasing the next four-legged meal every morning, we've farmed and grown to the phases of the moon. Thousands of years before Christ, across the Nile Delta farmers and growers used the moon as their guide to increase yields because their communities depended on it. The great Roman naturalist and philosopher Pliny the Elder (AD 23–79), author of *Naturalis Historia*, considered to be the founding father of what is now the modern encyclopedia, was no easy believer in received wisdom, yet he was a firm advocate of the effects of the moon on all living things.

It seems counterintuitive that multiple native American tribes, African cultures and aboriginal peoples, especially the Māoris, should reference the importance of the moon to food growing. You'd think ancient civilisations would concentrate on

THE NATURAL GARDENER

Pliny the Elder: 'That tiny creature the ant at the Moon's conjunction keeps quiet, but at the Full Moon works busily into the night . . . Geld hogs, steers, rams and kids when the Moon is waning.' – excerpts from *Naturalis Historia*

the sun and the weather when it comes to horticultural and husbandry advice. But time and again the moon is cited as a primary influence – not just as a mythological force, which you might expect, but as a celestial body that has practical, tangible influence on crop performance. The fact that it is cited so often and across so many cultures lends weight to, though not proof of, the idea that there's something going on here.

Of course, the advice and the mythologies don't always agree. In fact, they sometimes contradict each other on the specifics. But they all agree on one thing: the moon affects harvests and the behaviour of animals.

WHEN WE STOPPED MOVING, WE STARTED GROWING

This part of the book is a brief overview of some of these beliefs and some of the scientific research that has been conducted to test them, often with surprising results. It's by no means exhaustive and I encourage you to do your own research, keeping an open but sceptical mind as you do. In Part Four, you'll find useful links to further reading material in these areas.

21

How the Moon Helped those before us

THE MĀORIS

The Māoris are governed by a fundamental ethos that affects all aspects of their culture, and guides the delicate relationships among individuals, families, tribes and, perhaps most importantly of all, between humans and their immediate environment. It's called *Whakapapa* and, though hard to translate precisely, means 'a basis for the organisation of knowledge in the respect of the creation and development of all things' (from *Tikanga whakaaro: key concepts in Māori culture*, by Cleve Barlow, Oxford University Press, Auckland, New Zealand, 1994).

They believe everything has *Whakapapa*: all living and inanimate things, from specks of dust to mountains, microbes to whales, contain the history of what has happened before. How is

THE NATURAL GARDENER

THE MARAMATAKA

Night in the lunar cycle	Māori name	Māori advice
1	Whiro	The moon enters a new phase. An unfavourable day for planting food and for fishing. A good night for taking eel.
2	Tirea	A reasonably good night for crayfishing, eeling and planting food. A good day for collecting shellfish.
3	Hoata	A very good day for eeling, crayfishing, planting kūmara and sowing seed crops.
4	Ōue	A good day for establishing tuber beds, planting food and fishing.
5	Ōkoro	Another good day for planting food. Fish are restless.
6	Tamatea-kai ariki	A day for planting food. West winds prevail that only rain will quell.
7	Tamatea-ā ngana	Eels are voracious feeders this night. A good day for planting food and fishing, but beware fog and foaming sea.
8	Tamatea-āīō	Eel, fish and kūmara are abundant but small. A productive day for collecting shellfish. Fishermen, beware!
9	Tamatea-whakapau	A favourable day for planting food from morning to midday. Not very good for fishing.

HOW THE MOON HELPED THOSE BEFORE US

10	Ariro	A disagreeable day, one for marking time.
11	Huna	Do not plant food. Not a good day for fishing. Eel and crayfish are wary.
12	Māwharu	A most favourable day for planting food. Kūmara are large, but rot quickly. A good day for fishing; a good night for trapping crayfish and eel.
13	Ōhua	A very good day for planting food.
14	Atua whakahaehae	Not a good day for planting food or for fishing.
15	Ōturu	A good day for bobbing eel. A good day for fishing and for planting food from midday to sunset.
16	Rākaunui	A very good day. Crops are bountiful. A good day for fishing, but not eeling.
17	Rākaumatohi	A very good day for fishing, but not eeling. Seed plants grow vigorously.
18	Takirau	Takirau faintly visible. The moon is hazy. Food is bountiful, but small in size.
19	Ōike	Not a good day for fishing or for planting food.
20	Korekore-te-whiwhia	An unproductive night on the shore; winds sweep the seas.

21	Korekore-te-rawea	Not a fruitful night. Food is scarce, but await the turn of the tide.
22	Korekore-piri-ki Tangaroa	A good day from midday to sunset. A productive period for taking eel, trapped or otherwise. Most foods are plentiful.
23	Tangaroa-ā mua	A good day for planting food, for fishing and eeling.
24	Tangaroa-ā roto	Productive day for fishing and for planting food.
25	Tangaroa whakapau	A good day for fishing and the cultivation of seed beds.
26	Tangaroa-ā-kiokio	A very good day for taking eel, for fishing and for setting crayfish and eel baskets.
27	Ōtāne	A good day for fishing, eeling and crayfishing. A reasonably good day for planting food.
28	Ōrongonui	A very productive day for planting food, fishing and eeling.
29	Mauri	Not a productive day. Food is scarce. Fish are restless and turn tail.
30	Mutuwhenua	Unproductive day and night. The moon has diminished and the world is now in total darkness.

Names of days, and even the number of days in the calendar, varied from tribe to tribe. This table is based on those chosen by the Māori Language Commission as the names and system used by the majority of tribes.

HOW THE MOON HELPED THOSE BEFORE US

this relevant to Moon Gardening? As a result of *Whakapapa*, there's great reverence and respect given to resources (food) and the provider of those resources (land and sea). Māoris had, and still have, a deep cultural and practical connection with the land. For thousands of years tribes relied on knowledge passed down from elder to younger, generation to generation, for their survival and development.

At the centre of their horticultural thinking is the moon. Māoris plant to their own highly detailed moon calendar, known as the *Maramataka*. Though it varies from tribe to tribe, the *Maramataka* is a month- and day-specific guide for what to do throughout the year, according to how much of the moon is visible in the sky. It regulates planting, harvesting, fishing and hunting activities. The Māoris relied on and trusted the *Maramataka*, as a guide for good crops and catch, so over time, based on empirical observation, trial and error, the right times and days to grow, reap and gather were solidified into a system that produced reliable results.

For the Māoris, as with many cultures, the new moon marked the start of the lunar month, which was calculated at twenty-nine and a half days. Māoris didn't refer to days of the month, but rather nights, with Whiro the first and Mutuwhenua the last. As you can see in the table on page 174, certain nights were deemed unlucky for planting or harvesting or going out fishing; on others you were advised to make the most of the favourable moon conditions and plant, fish and reap away. (The moon was so central to Māori thinking that you see evidence of it everywhere, right down to their main agricultural tool – long-handled spades decorated with moon-crescent carvings.)

THE NATURAL GARDENER

In the past few decades, there has been a resurgence of interest in the science behind Māori horticultural techniques. Easy to dismiss as mythology and folklore, the thinking behind it is once again being taken seriously. Indeed, the Museum of New Zealand now dedicates considerable resources to explaining how the *Maramataka* shaped Māori society, and educating people on how to follow Māori Moon Gardening rules to get better results in their gardens.

If you ever visit New Zealand, take some time to visit Hamilton Gardens on North Island. It's home to Te Parapara, the only traditional Māori productive garden, which showcases the results of ancient agricultural practices, materials and

Traditional Māori Moon Gardening is used to grow bountiful crops of kūmara like these.

ceremonies dedicated to improving food production and storage. The techniques used are drawn from the knowledge of local Māori and often result in bumper crops of kumara (a delicious type of sweet potato).

NATIVE AMERICANS AND THE THREE SISTERS' PLANTING METHOD

When European settlers first arrived in the Americas in the early seventeenth century, they were intrigued by the growing traditions of the Iroquois people, who were able, from one patch of not-always-ideal ground, to produce three essential staples reliably every harvest: maize, squash and beans. Maize provided energy in carbohydrate; squash was a source of vital vitamins; and the beans were their main vegetable protein.

The three crops, revered as the Three Sisters, were always grown together and always in the same way. They nourished the tribes both physically and spiritually, because the method of planting was intrinsic to Iroquois folklore.

According to legend, the Three Sisters sprouted from the body of Sky Woman's daughter and gave the gift of agriculture to humans. The Three Sisters were all very different in character and appearance and, crucially, supported each other in different ways.

- Maize was the oldest and tallest sister, and therefore the one relied on to provide support for the others. The tall corn eliminates the need for poles: the beans climb up the corn.

- Squash was the next-oldest sister, the middle child, and protective of the other two. The large, prickly, sprawling leaves shade the ground from the harsh sun, provide a natural mulch when they die down, discourage weed growth and deter foraging animals like raccoons.

- Beans was the youngest and the giver of the three. The pole beans wind round the other two sisters, holding them close together and making them stronger. They also absorb nitrogen from the air and transfer it to the soil, benefiting every plant in the structure.

It's thought that the Iroquois had been practising this method for at least three hundred years before meeting the first white settlers.

The Iroquois believe that corn, beans and squash were precious gifts from the Great Spirit, watched over by the Three Sisters' spirits (called the De-o-ha-ko or 'Our sustainers'). To this day, the planting season begins with ceremonies that honour them, and the Green Corn Festival commemorates the first reaping of young corn on the cob – their equivalent of Thanksgiving. It's a system that also has a community message. If we stay and grow together, we thrive together. Work independently, we're less than the sum of our parts.

The tradition of interplanting corn, beans and squash in raised beds or mounds is actually common across numerous Native American farming societies. Maize, beans and squash were the first main crops nurtured by the ancient Mesoamerican societies. Corn was the versatile staple, providing more energy per acre than any other food known at the time. Beans were satisfying, filling and plentiful, while the many different types of squash added variety and flavour to what was at times, a near-subsistence diet. Recognition that they grew so well together and complemented each other organically resulted in a sustainable mini-ecosystem that encouraged fertile soil and provided a fulfilling, balanced diet for many generations of Native Americans in sometimes hostile growing environments.

In the US, many amateur gardeners and some organic farmers are turning to the Three Sisters method, regardless of their ancestry, partly because it works, but also because it is a way of feeling more connected to the long history of the land they live in.

Like the Māoris, Native Americans passed on their knowledge of growing, using and preserving the Three Sisters through storytelling and performing annual rituals. They, too, had discovered over time that some plants had a natural affinity for each other.

In the Western world, in the past hundred or so years, we've tended to scoff at folklore, dismissing so much as superstition and old wives' tales. It's an easy habit to fall into, but it's faulty thinking. I'm as guilty as the next. For years, my wife has said, 'You'll catch your death of cold, going out like that,' as I head for the door in shirt and trousers while the wind howls holes through the trees. And for years I've sighed and explained that being cold doesn't mean you'll *get* a cold. You need a virus to give you a cold, and there's been no scientific study showing any correlation between the two.

And then, in 2015, a group of Yale University scientists published a report showing that cold temperatures could weaken your immune system, thus making you much more vulnerable to picking up a virus. If you looked at it in a linear way, as many previous studies clearly had, being in the cold didn't *give* you a cold – of course it didn't, because cold didn't create the conditions for a thriving virus – but it did create the right environment for a cold to be more likely.

Companion planting is often dismissed in the same way – because it has its roots in mythology. Obviously, in 1300, the Iroquois didn't know the complex biochemistry behind the balanced nutritional breakdown of the corn, squash and beans they planted – but they did know, empirically, that it kept everyone in their tribe healthy, satisfied and full of energy. Nor could they have known the science behind the companion planting – how some plants absorb nitrogen and others leave it behind – but they did know, empirically, that when they planted them together they thrived, and when they planted them apart they only survived.

I've included the Three Sisters method here not because it has anything specifically to do with Moon Gardening (though, as with many aboriginal peoples the world over, the moon played a central role in Native American thinking and mythology), but more because it is an excellent example of a natural, traditional method of horticulture that is again in danger of being lost in the pursuit of the modern, for which you can often read the pursuit of profit.

Planting these crops using the Three Sisters method on a mass agricultural scale would be more time-consuming and labour-intensive, thus it would cost more. In monetary terms. But it saves so much that you can't put a price on: constant, self-replenishing, fertile soil; bountiful crops that are naturally resistant to pests and drought, but only when they are grown together; and that elusive, and I believe, priceless, connection to the land that develops a respect for the resources at our disposal.

I've also included it because it's really fun and productive to do in your own garden – kids, especially, love it because it combines great storytelling with easy-to-achieve results and extra-tasty food. Which child doesn't demolish buttery corn on the cob?

Throughout this book, you've read about methods for which, generously, one can say only that the jury's out scientifically. And while I'm always intrigued to know how and why things work – because such knowledge could help improve the methods I use in my garden – I'm not hung up on it. Though it would be gratifying, I don't need painstaking studies of my methodology to prove to me that what I do results in bigger, better crops, because the evidence is all around me. More importantly, I never hold the position that it's not worth pursuing something until it's proven to be beneficial. The best way to see if hearsay or old wives' tales or folklore is true is to test it yourself. If it works for you, there's nothing left to prove.

THE NATURAL GARDENER

BETTER BY NATURE: TIP #17
How to plant the Three Sisters in your garden

Outdoors, the Three Sisters method is suitable for gardeners in south and southwest UK only. With a large enough greenhouse, you might be able to adapt it to work under glass. Here's how to plant the Three Sisters in your garden, step by step.

1. Prepare the soil in spring, digging in fish fertiliser and potash in the moon's third and fourth quarters to increase fertility of the soil before you start.

2. Build a mound of soil 4 feet wide and 1 foot high.

3. When you're sure you've seen the last frost of the season, plant your corn in the mound, sowing kernels roughly 1 inch deep and about 1 foot apart in a circle. The circle should be about 2 feet wide.

4. Once your corn has grown to be about 5 inches high, plant four bean seeds evenly around the base of the stalks. About a week later, plant six squash seeds, evenly spaced, around the edge of the mound.

5. You can use the deep-trench method described in Part Two. If you do, keep each circle apart by at least 4 feet. The deep-trench method coupled with moon-gardening principles should eliminate, or at least

drastically reduce, the need for watering. But if you're not following these methods you will need to water in and make sure the soil stays moist until the corn, beans and squash take hold.

6. The pole beans should take 1–2 weeks to sprout. You'll need to train them onto the corn stalks to encourage them on their way. It does no harm to wrap them around a few times to give them the right idea.

7. Within a few weeks the squash leaves should spread out, providing essential cover and keeping the soil cool and moist.

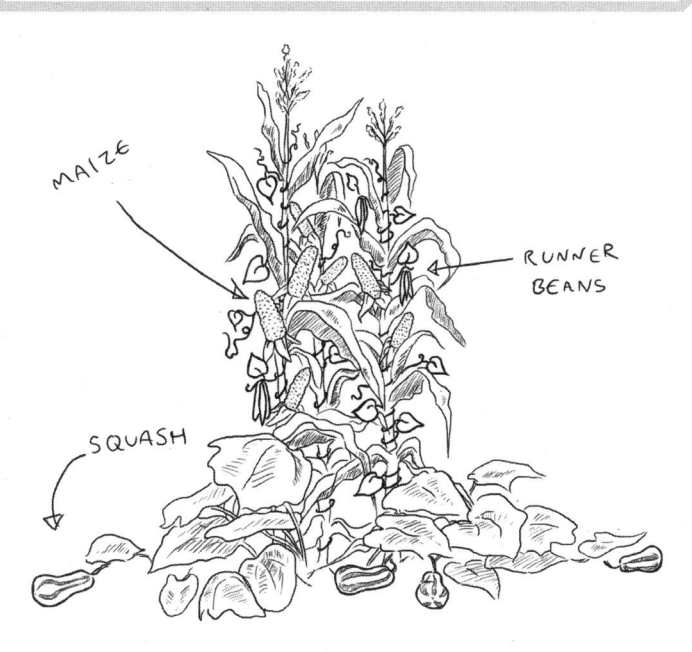

The Three Sisters method has been used for centuries to get plants to work together for the benefit of all involved.

22

Studies of the Moon's Effect on Plants

It has to be admitted that there aren't many hard-and-fast, repeatable experiments that prove the moon's influence on plants. Early-twentieth-century experiments after the flurry of interest triggered by the publication of Rudolph Steiner's controversial agricultural lectures in 1924 – which postulated that all living things were influenced by the position of the moon in relation to various astrological criteria – were to many observers inconclusive or ill-conceived.

However, there are some fascinating studies that have come out since the 1950s and right up to the present day that deserve further reading, either because they seem to have followed a more rigorous scientific method and are repeatable, or because they show interesting observations that point towards new areas of research into influences we don't yet understand. Here are some that have piqued my interest over the years.

THE 'THUN EFFECT': RUDOLPH STEINER AND BIODYNAMICS

Rudolf Steiner, the Austrian philosopher, published his (in)famous principles of biodynamics in 1924. He argued that there were life forces that connected all living things in the universe. On Earth, he argued that plant health was affected by the moon's energy. He believed deeply that sowing, pruning and harvesting in tune with lunar rhythms and patterns improved yield, flavour and pest resistance.

Not surprisingly, sceptics were as thick on the ground as weeds left untended – possibly because Steiner formulated his seemingly outlandish theories after apparently being informed of them telepathically by spirits.

So here's another case in kind. Though I don't dismiss it out of hand, I've never followed biodynamics. Maybe it's simple old me, but planting to the four quarters has improved my results so much over the years that I've never felt the need to observe the complex instructions of the biodynamic approach. But . . . something's happening to make it work for so many people who do go to the bother of learning it and putting it into practice. And the something that was happening, was put under rigorous test by Maria Thun in a series of famous experiments that the scientist-farmer started in the 1950s.

Thun began controlled trials with radishes. She planted them at different times, noted which constellation the moon was in and described the results over a period of many years. She discovered that the time of planting resulted not only in different levels of growth but also different forms. She concluded that onions,

STUDIES OF THE MOON'S EFFECT ON PLANTS

leeks and root crops benefited from being sown when the moon was passing through the earth-element constellations, flowering plants flourished under air signs, leafy plants responded best to the moon in water constellations, while fruits preferred fire signs. Her claims became known as the 'Thun effect'.

She used her findings to establish the thinking behind her horticultural approach in *Gardening for Life: the Biodynamic Way* (Hawthorn Press, 1999). Also worth a look is *When Wine Tastes Best 2015: A Biodynamic Calendar for Wine Drinkers* (Floris Books, 2015), which tells you the best days to taste wine. Again, this may be easy to laugh at, but some leading wine buyers for the supermarkets hold their tastings according to her principles.

ULF ABELE AND SIDEREAL MOON RHYTHMS

Note: sidereal refers to the 27.3-day lunar orbit. For a brief explanation of the difference between sidereal and synodic (29.5-day) months see 'Frequently Asked Questions' in Part Four.

Seeking to test the claims of the hotly disputed 'Thun effect' once and for all between 1970 and 1974, as part of his doctorate, Ulf Abele at Geissen University carried out meticulous, controlled research into whether crops were affected by moon rhythms. He tested grain crops (barley and oats) for the first two years, then followed up with root crops (carrots and radish) over the next two years. The barley and oats averaged an excess of 7 per cent better yield when planted on their appropriate moon sowing days, compared with controls planted over the same period.

Statistically significant but not earth-shattering. However, the carrots and radishes pulled their weight, showing an average 21 per cent yield increase.

What's important about these trials is that they were not one-offs. They initially set out to test the Thun effect, then Abele's trials in turn were retested by others in similar experiments. Between 1976 and 1998, Nicholas Kollerstrom and Gerhard Staudenmaier analysed potato-growing data from a Sussex farmer that showed a 30 per cent yield increase when they were sown on the correct 'root days'. Between 1979 and 1980, Lücke, also for his doctoral thesis, reported an 18 per cent yield increase in potatoes planted on 'root days' compared with controls planted on other days. In 1976, Ursula Graf devised a growth-chamber experiment that saw radishes grown on biodynamically treated soil showing a 20 per cent yield increase under what were termed 'very strict standardised experiments' in a review of the evidence by the Russian biologist A. P. Dubrov.

HOW THE MOON INFLUENCES THE BUILDING BLOCKS OF LIFE

In a fascinating experiment at the Sorbonne University, Paris, in 1990, lunar influence was examined at the most fundamental level of our lives: the behaviour of DNA structures. Using X-ray analysis, researchers documented changes over the synodic cycle. They found that carbohydrate storage structures were more developed at new moon while structures for flowering and growth were more developed at full moon. (Rossignol, M., et al., 'Lunar Cycle and Nuclear DNA Variations in Potato Callus', in *Geo-Cosmic Relations: The Earth and Its Macro-Environment,* ed. G. J. M. Tomassen, Wageningen, Netherlands 1990.)

PROFESSOR FRANK BROWN AND LUNAR-AFFECTED BIOLOGICAL RHYTHMS

Professor Frank A. Brown, of Northwestern University in Illinois, is worth a hefty mention here. Although over the course of his life his work was hotly debated and at times even shunned by his peers, he conducted some of the longest and most meticulous studies into the effects of the moon on marine life and crops.

Brown was fascinated by describing, testing and explaining patterns and cycles within living organisms. He was rigorous in his approach, spending years establishing controls and uncompromised laboratory conditions. His studies were many, and a quick Google search will give you all the further reading you may need, but I'm going to mention just two here.

The first was his famous work in the early 1970s investigating how oysters open and close valves in tune with the tides. Brown wanted to test whether oysters were genuinely reading both local conditions and the lunar cycles or whether some other forces were at play. So he arranged for a shipment of healthy Long Island oysters to be transported to Chicago, Illinois. To avoid any interference from daylight, they were kept completely in the dark while in transit.

For two weeks after settling into their new home, the oysters kept doing what they had always done: opening and closing their valves according to the rise and fall of the Long Island tides. But, over time, Brown noticed that the oysters' habits were changing. They started to reset their 'tidal clocks' even though they were still under lab conditions. Soon their valves were responding to what would have been an Illinois tide timetable, even though Chicago's coastline is of course Lake Michigan, a landlocked body of water with no tides. In plain words, they had shifted their feeding cycles in line with the lunar cycle.

How did they know where they were without any environmental clues? Even after years of research Brown didn't come to a firm conclusion, but he did prove that oysters, like many other living things, responded to lunar cycles themselves, not just the effects of lunar cycles on other bodies (such as the sea).

The second was another groundbreaking study, again notable for the sheer scale and exhaustiveness of the experiment. He stored potatoes in the dark under carefully controlled conditions, regulating humidity, pressure and temperature. Monitoring the equivalent of more than a million potato hours proportional to metabolism, he found that the metabolic rate and oxygen absorption of the potatoes rose and fell with the waxing and waning of the moon. In a similar study, also conducted under strict conditions at the Northwestern University ('Lunar-correlated variations in water uptake by bean seeds, *Biological Bulletin*, October 1973), he demonstrated that pinto beans absorbed 35 per cent more water around full moon compared with new moon. These findings were repeated in a 1976 study by Dr Jane Panzer at Tulane University, New Orleans ('Correlated Variations in Water Uptake and Germination in 3 Species of Seeds', PhD thesis, Tulane University).

23

Studies of the Moon's Effect on Animals (Including Us)

We've all heard the stories of dogs acting strangely, and increased violence reported by UK police forces every full moon. And many of us will have heard the immediate refutation by commentators who point to many studies that dismiss cases as apocryphal or results being distorted by the bias of those compiling data. Indeed, I've listened patiently to many people, including scientists in TV debates, saying there has never been a study showing any evidence that the moon affects our bodies or our behaviour, other than the generally agreed effects of increased activity for example due to moonlight (when the sky is not overcast).

To which I say, there have been numerous scientific studies showing some correlation between lunar cycles and animal behaviour, at both micro- and macro-levels. There's a species of rabbitfish, the streamlined spinefoot (*Siganus argenteus*), living in the shallow waters of the Indo-Pacific, whose hormone levels in its testes change to the rhythm of the moon, meaning it nearly always spawns around the fourth quarter (M Zimecki,: 'The Lunar cycle: effects on human and animal behavior and physiology', *Postepy Hig Med Dosw*, 2006.

Honeybees' bodyweight reaches its maximum at new moon. Every summer, The coral *Platygyra lamellina*, in the Red Sea, spawns during a 3–5-day period around the new moon in July and August. (This is particularly interesting, because many studies have shown corals in other parts of the world becoming more active during full moon – understandably attributed to more nocturnal light increasing what is known as 'synchronised spawning' – so what's happening in the Red Sea?)

'MOON MADNESS' – FACT OR FICTION?

In a *Guardian* article (5 June 2007), Sussex police claimed that they had tracked clear rises in aggressive behaviour among drinkers on the streets of Brighton around the time of the full moon. Acting on the research, senior officers deployed more officers in the following months to counter the increased violence they believed was linked to the lunar cycle.

Inspector Andy Parr explained:

> 'I compared a graph of full moons and a graph of last year's violent crimes and there is a trend. People tend to be more aggressive . . . From my experience, over nineteen years of being a police officer, undoubtedly

STUDIES OF THE MOON'S EFFECT ON ANIMALS (INCLUDING US)

on full moons, we do seem to get people with stranger behaviour – more fractious, argumentative. And I think that's something that's been borne out by police officers up and down the country for years.'

This is not an isolated study. In 1998, 1,200 inmates at Leeds's Armley jail were monitored over a course of three months and, again, a clear rise in violent incidents was noted during the days either side of the full moon.

Sadly, the RSPCA concurs. For years, it had noticed spikes in phone calls reporting animal abuse during full moons. In 2014, when it started to track the data and compare it with the lunar cycle, it found that there was an average increase of 12 per cent around the full moon. Staff Officer Dermot Murphy said, 'We can't explain why this phenomenon occurs, although there are anecdotal reports from emergency services that they also see an increase.'

It's a belief held by services across the globe. In January 2008, New Zealand's Justice Minister, Annette King, linked a spike in violence to the lunar effect, while back in 1978 the University of Washington published the results of a five-year study that examined 11,613 cases of aggravated assault, clearly showing a rise around full moon.

Perhaps the most controversial and famous study of linking madness to the lunar phases was Arnold Lieber's book, *The Lunar Effect: Biological Tides and Human Emotions*. In it, the psychiatrist studied violent human behaviour in major US cities. He analysed rates of murder, aggravated assault, suicide, psychiatric emergencies and fatal car accidents, and showed that they clearly increased and decreased in line with moon phases. Though hotly contested by scientists at the time, the book was a runaway bestseller because it reflected people's anecdotal and personal experiences. It's still widely available from Amazon and other sellers and is worth a read.

PROFESSOR MICHAEL ZIMECKI

It's not *all* about violence and madness. In his comprehensive collation of new research and a review of fifty other studies, Professor Michael Zimecki of the Polish Academy of Sciences looks at the proposed links between the phase of the moon and the workings of the human body. Here's a quick taster of some of the most interesting stats.

According to Leeds University, GP consultations go up during a full moon with appointments rising by 3.6 per cent (an extra three patients per surgery). In New York City, 140,000 births were monitored, showing a small but regular peak in fertility during the third quarter. The report concluded: 'The timing of the fertility peak in the third quarter suggests that the period of decreasing illumination immediately after the full moon may precipitate ovulation.'

In another study, eight hundred patients with urinary retention problems were monitored over three years, and it was found that they achieved higher retention during the new moon compared with the rest of the lunar cycle.

And at Georgia State University, they found that nutrient intake and meal patterns were affected by lunar variations, concluding: 'A small but significant lunar rhythm of nutrient

STUDIES OF THE MOON'S EFFECT ON ANIMALS (INCLUDING US)

intake was observed with an 8 per cent increase in meal size and a 26 per cent decrease in alcohol intake at the time of the full moon relative to the new moon.'

What's happening here? According to Zimecki, the moon may be a catalyst for hormonal changes:

> The lunar cycle has an impact on human reproduction, in particular fertility, menstruation and birth rate. Other events associated with human behaviour, such as traffic accidents, crimes, and suicides, appeared to be influenced by the lunar cycle . . .
>
> Although the exact mechanism of the moon's influence on humans and animals awaits further exploration, knowledge of this kind of biorhythm may be helpful in police surveillance and medical practice . . .
>
> At this stage of investigation, the exact mechanism of the lunar effect on the immune response is hard to explain. The prime candidates to exert regulatory function on the immune response are melatonin and steroids, whose levels are affected by the Moon cycle . . . It is suggested that melatonin and endogenous steroids may mediate the described cyclic alterations of physiological processes.

SURGERY AND AMPUTATIONS

It's only in the past century that people have ridiculed the old idea that the human body heals better during certain lunar phases. Yet, as mentioned in Chapter 11, right up to the First World War amputations were delayed until a waning moon, because for centuries surgeons observed empirical evidence that outcomes were improved when they followed certain lunar phases.

Now it seems they were right after all. Research published in the *Journal of Interactive Cardiovascular and Thoracic Surgery* in 2013 for Rhode Island Hospital in the USA revealed that surgery, especially for correcting acute aortic dissection, resulted in a lower death rate when the moon was waning. Researchers tracked variations on survival rates and length of hospital stay following heart surgery. Senior author Dr Frank Sellke said:

> While there's been previous research on the seasonal impacts of cardiovascular disease, there has not been any data about the effect of the lunar cycles on cardiac cases, until now. We focused the study on patients having aortic dissection and found that the odds of dying following this procedure were greatly reduced during the waning full moon, and that length of stay was also reduced during the full moon.

So, if you're having heart surgery, ask for it to take place after the full moon.

24

Last Thoughts

Today we live in world that exists around material assets. Our lives are often hectic with little time to think about the cycles we live through and their impact on us and the natural world around us. Most of us shop in supermarkets and eat the food from them. It is a far cry from the lifestyle of the old Native American ways. For many Native American tribes, such as the Hopi and Navajo, observing the cycles of life, including the lunar cycles, was essential for their existence. One area in which the observations of the moon and planets were significant was agriculture. Today we can gain useful insight into a healthier lifestyle by observing the some of the traditional ways of Native American peoples because their way of life is particularly significant as many of us have chosen to turn to a more natural way of living. This way of life may include growing our own fruit and veg. For many of us this is an important move towards liberation away from living in an ever-growing, consumer-driven world.

It's easy to dismiss traditional belief as superstition. Sometimes, that's all it is, but often there's a nugget of truth behind the belief, especially when it comes to practical advice that helped us have an easier life. Our grandmothers and grandfathers, and theirs before them, all had a bank of knowledge that helped them achieve more for less, because resources were scarcer.

Many years ago, when I was presenting at the Chelsea Flower Show, I met a distant relative of the Sioux Indians, now a professor at Wyoming University. We ended up talking for hours about the moon. It reignited my fascination with how cultures throughout history and across the globe had used the moon and been affected by it.

In the early 1980s a New Zealand TV production company came over to Tresillian to interview me about Moon Gardening and I distinctly remember a producer muttering to his assistant, 'I don't know why we travelled twelve thousand miles – the Māoris have been doing this for thousands of years!'

The moon crops up as having influences in all manner of places. In an online forum linked to 'lunar hair cutting', I saw this post:

> I have used the moon phases to trim and grow my beard for several years now. When initially growing my beard out I only trimmed it on the days that the moon was growing or waxing as they call it. I ended up growing a 10 to 12-inch beard in a year's time. Now I trim it just after the full moon in the spring to slow the growth down for the summer and with 2 weeks after the new moon to start the faster growth cycle up for

the winter. Now there are three other men here at work that are following the same cycles and everyone keeps asking why we are able to grow our beards out so much faster. So yes, following the moon phase does work. The sad thing is that we have so many young 'know it all' intellectuals giving their professional, untried, opinions that we are losing the good things that people have lived by for thousands of years.

MOON-POWERED TRADING?

The more you investigate the moon's influence in all areas of our lives, the more you find it's not a load of mumbo-jumbo. There's even a fascinating correlation between lunar phases and stock trading, as successful trader Vincent Troncone discovered.

It's such an interesting article, I wanted to reproduce it in its entirety here, but, unfortunately, I've been unable to track down Mr Troncone to ask his permission. So all I'll say is that he has found what appears to be a direct correlation between the primary phases of the moon and the points at which any given, freely traded market will reverse direction. He claims it's a phenomenon that has nothing to do with astrology and everything to do with astronomy and physics.

You can read the full text of 'Trading by the light of the Moon' at http://www.moonconnection.com/moon_trading.phtml

THE NATURAL GARDENER

As you read this, the moon is moving away from us. Each year, the moon steals some of Earth's rotational energy, and uses it to propel itself about 1.6 inches (4 centimetres) higher in its orbit.

Researchers say that, when it formed about 4.6 billion years ago, the moon was about 14,000 miles (22,530 kilometres) from Earth. It's now more than 280,000 miles (450,000 kilometres) away.

Moon Gardening as a practice was almost eclipsed by the mid-twentieth century, and, apart from the efforts of a few, it might well have disappeared altogether as a source of knowledge. The truth is, no matter how crazy you might think it sounds, it works. The proof is in the planting. And the pruning. And the reaping.

I've studied many types of horticulture and been exposed to all manner of commercial gardening methods from big garden centres to estate management. None of the additives, the miracle growth compounds, the pesticides and chemical fertilisers can touch the natural power of the moon.

In talks, I've been lucky to be able to retrace the steps of our forefathers and show people of today how successful our ancestors were without any recourse to modern facilities. And what always surprises my audiences is when I say, 'You don't have to go back too far to see what we're losing.' Just before the First World War, farming to lunar cycles was the way of life, whether you were in private service or owned your own garden – a few chickens, a small plot to support your family (often larger than families are today). Animals were slaughtered according to the right time of the moon. Many's the time I heard as a child old men say, 'You can't do that – the moon ain't right.'

LAST THOUGHTS

My aim in this book was always to bring to your attention a way of life that was commonplace before the world sped up. The gardening that our ancestors followed was vital; it was inextricably linked to their immediate surroundings and there was a mutually beneficial relationship between the tiller and the tilled. We are in danger of losing connection with the world around us at a fundamental level. That's why I always say to people, 'Tread lightly on the earth because it's the food basket of tomorrow.'

My wonderful gardening mentor, Noel Masters, said before he passed away, 'Promise me, John, that one day you'll study the art of Moon Gardening.' He'd been head gardener at Polwhele for most of his life and, though in his early years he'd followed the traditional methods that his father and his father's father had taught him, over time he'd felt the pressure and indeed the necessity to adapt to the commercial drive for bigger, more, better, faster. Gardening was his passion, but it was also his business and, in the early postwar rush to throw out the old and embrace the new, Noel followed suit. There was nothing wrong with this, and you should face the world with an open mind or not bother at all, but I did feel that, in the later parts of his life, there may have been some regret that he'd been swept up in the drive for modernity.

So, when he asked, it was easy for me to say, 'Yes.' I made the promise, and though it took me a fair few years to get started – and I had no idea of the scale of the task I had vowed to complete – now, fifty years later, I have seen the incredible abundance that can be achieved through gardening by the phases of the moon. I have no regrets and no doubts. But I do still have a lot to learn.

Part Four: Appendixes

Grow What You Know, Know What You Grow

Develop deep-rooted knowledge, watch your garden flourish, share what you learn

Appendix I

Useful Resources

Keeping your ground fertile is all about using your resources well, which means feeding your brain as well as your land. I'm a firm believer that the best tool we have is shared knowledge. So here are some of the most useful the things I know, and the places I go to for the things I don't.

ALLOTMENTS

Where to apply for an allotment: https://www.gov.uk/apply-allotment

Great general allotment advice: http://www.nsalg.org.uk/allotment-info/how-to-get-an-allotment/

THE NATURAL GARDENER

Green your city – get an allotment.

COLORADO MOON GARDENING

https://www.growveg.co.uk/garden-plans/480269/elizabeth-colorado/2014/lisas-garden/

No, this isn't some factional split from the original proponents of Moon Gardening. Rather, it is an information-packed site run by Lisa Montrose, who has produced amazing results in the hard-pan soil in Colorado, dramatically reducing water usage by 40 per cent while hugely improving the quality and quantity of her crops.

Over the years, Lisa has been a wonderful supporter of my

gardening approach and a great friend. I'm extremely grateful for her support. She has much to add on the subject.

COMPOSTS

http://www.johninnes.info/

The only type of bought composts I use are John Innes, because you just can't go wrong with them. I tend to use only numbers 1 to 3. You should aim to buy peat-free and 100 per cent organic so you know they'll never harm your garden – or anyone else's.

Grade	Purpose
Sowing	Sowing seeds and rooting cuttings
No. 1	Sowing large seeds and pricking out
No. 2	Potting up and potting on
No. 3	Final potting
Ericaceous	For your lime-haters

People often think John Innes is a manufacturer, but actually he was a Victorian landowner and property developer who bequeathed his fortune to horticultural research. The result is a series of wonderful composts designed for very specific purposes.

Good organic reliable brands of John Innes composts include GroWise and Vital Earth.

THE NATURAL GARDENER

HERITAGE FOOD

https://www.gardenorganic.org.uk/hsl

Once they're gone, they're gone. This isn't a special offer. We need to look after our horticultural history by nurturing all the dead ends and by-products of seed development and breeding. Besides, it's fun and you end up growing and eating plants no one else has heard of. Above is a great site, of an important organisation doing wonderful work. Have a good browse of Garden Organic's Heritage Seed Library.

Heritage seeds – do you have any?

If you have seeds that you're not sure how to grow properly, please do contact me at Tresillian. In our kitchen garden we've nurtured plants to full growth from seeds sent to us from all around the world. I'm always happy to advise or help where I can. You can email me on: rjohn.harris8@btinternet.com

MOON CALENDARS: ONLINE

http://www.calendar-365.co.uk/moon/moon-calendar.html

A brilliant online moon calendar for the UK with a photographic representation of the phase of the moon, day by day up to one year ahead. (For easy reference, please also see my moon calendars for 2020 to 2022 printed at the end of the book.)

USEFUL RESOURCES

http://www.moonconnection.com/moon_phases_calendar.phtml

Our old friend MoonConnection again. This is a world moon calendar that calculates based on the time zone set by your computer.

MOON GARDENING: SCIENTIFIC STUDIES AND ARTICLES

As we saw in Chapters 22 and 23, this is a controversial area. Many studies show a beneficial correlation between the phases of the moon, many don't. In the end, all I ask is that you try it and judge for yourself. I hope that, after putting into practice what I've preached, you'll feel the same. But, in case you're still making up your mind, here are some links to some eye-opening studies:

http://www.astro-calendar.com/shtml/Research/research_Kollerstrom2.shtml (detailed analysis of Maria Thun's and later related trials)

New Zealand Herald, 'How the Moon rules your life' by Roger Dobson (superb overview of recent research including the substantial work of Professor Michael Zimecki)
http://www.nzherald.co.nz/science/news/article.cfm?c_id=82&objectid=10420153

MOON-PHASE TRADING

Can the moon make you money? There are professional foreign exchange traders who use it to predict fluctuations in currency. Check out these links:

YouTube video: Moon Phase Trader: https://www.youtube.com/watch?v=6Q-l5n7i8AQ&feature=youtu.be

Vincent Troncone: 'Trading by the Light of the Moon': http://www.moonconnection.com/moon_trading.phtml

OTHER EFFECTS: SCIENTIFIC STUDIES AND ARTICLES

As we have seen, folklore, mythology and anecdotes abound with tales of the moon affecting humans, animals and even the stock market. Below are a few links to some of my favourite studies and articles on the subject:

Ulf Abele, 'Saatzeitversuche mit Radies'., *Lebendige Erde* 6, pp. 223–5, 1975

Morrocco Method of Hair Cutting: http://www.morroccomethod.com/blog/cutting-hair-by-the-moon/

Latest surgery research: http://www.dailymail.co.uk/health/article-2365941/Having-heart-surgery-Make-sure-FULL-

MOON--Heart-surgery-patients-recover-quicker-certain-lunar-phases.html

ORGANIC ORGANISATIONS AND RESOURCES

The Soil Association is the UK's leading membership charity campaigning for healthy, humane and sustainable food, farming and land use.

Soil Association
South Plaza
Marlborough Street
Bristol BS1 3NX
0117 314 5000
www.soilassociation.org/

Numerous email and contact details here: http://www.soilassociation.org/aboutus/contactus

Organic Farmers & Growers (OF&G) is a leading UK organic control body with a reputation for practical, efficient and friendly service. Talk to it about the inspection and licensing of organic food processing, farming, body-care products and other organic enterprises.

THE NATURAL GARDENER

Old Estate Yard
Shrewsbury Road
Albrighton
Shrewsbury SY4 3AG
01939 291800
http://www.organicfarmers.org.uk/
email: info@ofgorganic.org

The following sites are packed with great advice and further resources and are well worth visiting:

http://www.gardenorganic.org.uk

en.wikipedia.org/wiki/Organic_horticulture

http://www.rhs.org.uk/advice (put 'organic' in the search box for reliable articles on the subject)

http://www.motherearthnews.com/organic-gardening (includes an interesting crop-by-crop guide to growing – worth a dip)

http://www.verdant.net/food.htm (not the easiest of sites on the eye but it is passionately written and full of detailed advice on growing food organically for your family)

USEFUL RESOURCES

SEED SUPPLIERS

Below are the individuals and firms I buy my seeds from. They are all friendly to deal with and completely reliable. Many of them deal in unusual varieties, including heritage seeds, and all are happy to discuss your needs and help you find what you're looking for.

Thomas Etty
Seedsmans Cottage
Puddlebridge
By Ilminster
Somerset TA19 9RL
01460 298249
http://www.thomasetty.co.uk
email: sales@thomasetty.co.uk

Kings Seeds
Monks Farm
Pantlings Lane
Coggeshall Road
Essex CO5 9PG
01376 570 000
http://www.kingsseeds.com
email: info@kingsseeds.com

THE NATURAL GARDENER

Real Seed Catalogue
PO Box 18
Newport
Pembrokeshire SA65 0AA
01239 821107
http://www.realseeds.co.uk/
email: info@realseeds.co.uk

Edwin Tucker
Brewery Meadow,
Stonepark,
Ashburton
Newton Abbott TQ13 7DG
01364 652233
http://www.edwintucker.co.uk/seeds/
email: seeds@edwintucker.com

Plants of Distinction
Abacus House
Station Yard
Needham Market
Suffolk IP6 8AS
Orders: 01206 307999
Customer Service: 01449 721720
http://www.plantsofdistinction.co.uk
email: sales@plantsofdistinction.co.uk

USEFUL RESOURCES

Chiltern Seeds
Crowmarsh Battle Barns
114 Preston Crowmarsh
Wallingford OX10 6SL
01491 824675
http://www.chilternseeds.co.uk
info@chilternseeds.co.uk

Tresillian Estate
Tresillian House
Near Newquay
Cornwall TR8 4PS
http://www.tresillianhouse.co.uk
07771 782 202

Over the past quarter of a century, Tresillian Estate has allowed me the opportunity to pursue and test my belief in Moon Gardening. The current owner, George Robinson, offers the house out for holiday accommodation and the estate and kitchen garden is occasionally opened to horticultural societies for tours.

Appendix II

Further Reading

Sorry for the plug, but there isn't a great deal of literature on Moon Gardening itself, so I'm going to mention a couple of books I wrote a few years ago. At the time of going to press, they were both out of print (but we're working on it). They have the same title, but the first and second editions have quite different content. You can probably find them on eBay or Amazon.

R J Harris with Will Summers, *Moon Gardening* (1st edn) Shrewsbury, Shropshire, Really Useful Books, 2002
ISBN: 0-9542394-0-7

R J Harris with Will Summers, *Moon Gardening* (2nd edn) Shrewsbury, Shropshire, Really Useful Books, 2007
ISBN: 978-0-9542394-1-1

I may be biased because I'm honoured to have been included

in it, but the following book is probably the best book about the relationship between your garden and your kitchen that's been published in the past twenty years. Essential reading for everyone concerned about the state of the food on their plate, but inspired by the possibilities of new and exciting plants and flavours we can all know grow in our own back gardens. The title alone makes me want to get back out there!

Mark Diacono, *The New Kitchen Garden: How to Grow Some of What You Eat No Matter Where You Live*
London, Saltyard Books, 2015
ISBN 978-1-44473-478-2

See Mark's website too:
http://www.otterfarm.co.uk/the-new-kitchen-garden

I have to give a plug to a book that isn't really about Moon Gardening at all, but is so full of useful advice about household and gardening tips – all traditional and all organic – that I couldn't resist sharing.

Alex Goffey, *The Traditional Household Handbook*
Windsor Books, 2012
ISBN: 978-1-90390-482-4

The following are permanently on my office (a.k.a. glorified garden shed) shelf. If you're lucky enough to come across any one of them in a jumble sale or charity shop, buy it. They are all inspirational, beautiful books and packed with practical advice.

FURTHER READING

John Weathers, *My Garden Book*
London, Longmans, Green & Co., 1924

Alexander L Howard, *Trees in Britain and their Timbers*
London, Country Life Ltd, 1947

J C Loudon, *An Encyclopaedia of Plants*
London, Longmans, Green & Co., 1829

W E Shewell-Cooper, *The Complete Gardener*
London, Collins, 1940

N P Harvey, *Encyclopaedia of Modern Gardening*
London, Spring Books, 1961

Appendix III

Frequently Asked Questions

It's a strange old subject, Moon Gardening. I've tried in this book to cover all the basics and bring in other complementary techniques so that you can get the best out of your garden. It's impossible to answer every question that comes up but I've done my best below to answer the ones I hear most frequently. If your questions aren't answered here, please don't hesitate to email me at j.harris670@btinternet.com and I'll get back to you as soon as I can.

Q: What's a blue moon?

A: The term 'blue moon' used to have many different meanings, but since the middle of last century it has come to mean the relatively rare occurrence of two full moons in one month, the second one being the blue moon. This happens roughly every three years, hence the term 'once in a blue moon'.

Q: Are there any rarely used heritage varieties of herbs available from seed sellers? Do you know of any herbs that used to be commonly used but have fallen out of fashion?

A: Ninety per cent of our herbs were brought in by the Romans and are still used today. There are herbs used around the world that you rarely see here, often because the assumption is they won't grow here. But, as Mark Diacono advocates in his brilliant book *The New Kitchen Garden*, there's no reason not to try. We have a temperate climate and you can always grow under glass, or try to replicate unusual soil conditions.

You can also explore the herbs you think you already know. For instance, there are thirty different types of basil and almost endless variations of mint – strawberry, red, pineapple, chocolate – and rarer types of sage such as purple, red and grey sage. A personal favourite of mine that few people seem to know about is strawberry stick, which produces minute strawberry fruits. Eat the leaves like spinach – absolutely delicious.

Q: You claim not to water your garden for irrigation purposes. But what if the water table is really low? Did you really not water in the drought of 1976?

A: I wasn't at Tresillian at the time, but I really didn't. One of the secrets of Moon Gardening is that it uses natural forces to your advantage. I use deep trenching to capture that force as much as possible. Deep trenches act as a sponge and work very effectively for about four years, before they're used up and need to be replenished. They are layered with feed but also drier matter that helps draw in moisture and hold it when the water table is rising.

In times of environmental stress my plants carry on happily because they have an ever-ready supply of water and nutrients that have been captured by the moon-powered rise of the water table. So, in the case of the 1976 drought, even though there was no water coming from above and the water table itself had fallen dramatically below my deep trenches, the soil had previously tapped moisture from the rise and fall of the water table and held it long enough to keep my garden happy.

There are of course many other techniques for preserving moisture in the ground, some of which I talk about in detail in this book. One worth mentioning in times of extreme conditions is mulching with leaf mould. Bag up leaves in the autumn and layer your ground when it gets too dry. Your plants will love you for it.

Q: Do I have to garden at night, in the dark?

A: No. Although a few gardeners swear by it, I don't believe the extra hassle is worth the possible increase in quality and taste. If you want to go out at night, however, feel free. I prefer to be indoors by then, resting weary legs and sinking into my settee, because I spend literally all day in the garden.

Q: What happens if I miss a date or I harvest a few days too late or early?

A: Nothing. The sky won't fall in and you won't be told off.

Gardening is chaos theory in action. There are so many variables that you can offset the negatives of one action by adopting another one to alleviate it. Moon Gardening works very well, but so do many other types of gardening.

The specific answer to the question is that your fruit or vegetables will be less tasty and juicy than they could have been if you'd followed everything to a T for optimum results. But they'll still be a damn site better than most of the stuff in the shops.

I want you to enjoy your gardening, not stress out about adopting everything I advocate here. We all have busy lives and competing demands on our time. The more you follow Moon Gardening principles, the better your results will be, but it is all incremental, rather than all or nothing. So, do what you can, when you can, and enjoy it.

Q: What's the evidence for following Moon Gardening?

A: Every time I step out into Tresillian's kitchen garden, the evidence smacks me in the face. Follow the principles and you'll see it in your own garden, too. And herein lies the problem. Most of the evidence is anecdotal and empirical rather than subject to rigorous scientific testing. I've conducted my own tests. Every year, side by side, I plant some potatoes in accordance with the lunar phases and some deliberately out of sync. The out-of-sync plantings are significantly smaller and less tasty. The evidence really is there for all to see (and taste!). There are no double blinds and controls and any scientist worth their salt would say there may be bias in the way I go about my tests. I understand the scepticism but don't agree with it.

FREQUENTLY ASKED QUESTIONS

However, it really is time some thorough, long-term testing was done to settle the argument once and for all, because it's quite possible that I've seen huge success due to the combination of some of my methods with Moon Gardening principles, which is why I've placed a lot of emphasis in this book on marrying lunar phases with other traditional methods for best results.

None of which specifically answers the question. There have been some studies over the past hundred years. I go into detail in Part Three about a few of them. Some have shown no correlation, others have shown clear improvements. (I blame the multiple variables involved.)

The most extensive work was done by Maria Thun back in the 1950s. A German researcher, she published a number of comparative Moon Gardening trials following the biodynamic Moon Gardening techniques (this is slightly different from my more simplified, less 'astrological' approach).

More recently the BBC's *A Year at Kew Gardens* (broadcast in 2007) showed clear success for Moon Gardening methods in comparative trials conducted under scientifically supervised conditions.

Q: If Moon Gardening worked so well, why did the practice die out?

A: Good question, and key to understanding the demise of traditional methods of husbandry and agriculture the world over. It died out because modern methods, using intensive farming and superpowered fertilisers, completely overshadowed the more subtle effects of planting by the moon. For many people, it made them irrelevant altogether. Aided chemically, you can get big, unblemished plants out of season. But you'll lose out in taste and nutrition, and in the long term your soil, and all our soils, will be damaged. Moon Gardening, traditional methods and organic gardening can produce spectacular results as long as you don't fight nature. We're only just rediscovering this after more than fifty years of constantly chasing the next chemical or technical horticultural development.

Q: What are sidereal and synodic months? What's the difference between them?

A. As simply as possible, a sidereal month is the time the moon takes to orbit the earth relative to the distant background stars (*sidereus* being the Latin for 'relating to stars'), which takes 27.32 days. The effect of the earth's orbit of the sun, however, means that it actually takes the moon longer – 29.53 days – to travel round the earth from one new moon to the next. This period is the synodic (from the Greek for 'meeting') or lunar month and is the basis for our familiar monthly calendar.

Q: Is the moon the biggest influence on my garden?

A: Absolutely not – *you* are. The weather, fertilisers, choice of seeds and general care and attention all obviously play a huge part, too. But, if you get the fundamentals right, then bring in Moon Gardening techniques, you'll see a significant further improvement. Your yields should increase by a minimum of 10 per cent (it can be much more) and the taste will be noticeably better. As important, get it right and you'll be doing less watering in the garden and paying less because you don't have to use so much feed.

Q: Can Moon Gardening mitigate bad weather?

A: Sometimes, a little. As with previous answers, practical considerations often override the subtler effects of the moon. Nowhere does Moon Gardening dictate that you go out and sow during a thunderstorm. The elements take first priority and you may find yourself having to abandon Moon Gardening timings just to get your crop in safely. However, follow planting by the lunar phases and you'll find your plants crop better, your garden is generally fitter and all will be able to withstand the elements that bit better.

Q: Why does Moon Gardening work?

A: From my own observations I think it's mainly down to the water table and probably increased insect and bacterial activity, but the jury's still out. Nobody really knows – the evidence is mixed and sometimes conflicting. Differing amounts of reflected light from the moon, the gravitational pull of the moon on fluids within plants, the water table affected by the moon's pull, even variations in magnetic fields, distorted by the moon at apogee and perigee – all these been mooted. Something's happening, but nobody's exactly sure what it is yet.

THE NATURAL GARDENER

Q: Why is your Moon Gardening calendar different from others?

A: I've always followed a really simple system of working to the four quarters of the moon. There are many other systems out there, including biodynamic gardening, that place emphasis on star signs, conjunctions, etc. I don't hold to that. I am simply passing on to you what has worked for me. And it's easy to follow, which helps an old man like me.

Q: Should I garden during an eclipse?

A: If you want to. You might bump into things, though. It gets quite dark.

Coda: New Moon

A FEW HOPES

I hope I've bedded in OK after all these years here at Tresillian. I know the kitchen garden and the estate are bedded in with the community. It seems like most people put up with the loony now. Sticking to the vision has worked, and it brought great rewards for me personally – though maybe not financially, does anyone know a good agent? – and it helped raise the profile of the estate enormously.

I hope, too, that I haven't sounded as though I've been on my old soapbox again. Even my friends say I sometimes have a one-track mind. I just want people to know about this for their own sakes. I feel a duty to share this knowledge because it is so simple to follow and offers such great benefits. But, if people don't believe it, that's genuinely fine. You have to agree to differ in life. My beautiful wife, Olive, thinks her pasties are OK. I beg to differ – they're the best I've ever tasted (and the co-author of this book thinks so too). Everyone has a right to their own opinion, no matter how wrong it is.

And I hope I'm not one of those sour old allotment stereotypes who grump at any new invention or hark back with a hair-shirt view of life to a golden age of horses and ploughs. I'm a very firm believer that there's more than one way to skin a cat, eat at table, or plant a row of beans. There is never one single correct answer to any problem. I just happen to know that my way produces more for less cost – and it's fun! Which is what gardening should be: therapeutic, healthy, story-generating and life-affirming. It should make you smile.

All I'm asking of you is to take a step back. You've learned the modern way and it's fine. It feeds the world – at least it should – and it gets us all to where we need to be faster. But, and it's a big but, I was given a chance to turn the clock back and show what our ancestors did using only what was around them.

It worked for them, it works for me, and it will work for you. So, finally, I hope this book has inspired you just to give it a try, and see what happens when you plant and reap to the persuasive pull of the relentless moon.

My 2020–2022 Moon Gardening Calendars

2020 MOON CALENDAR

New Moon	First Quarter	Full Moon	Last Quarter
	3rd January	10th January	17th January
24th January	2nd February	9th February	15th February
23rd February	2nd March	9th March	16th March
24th March	1st April	8th April	14th April
23rd April	30th April	7th May	14th May
22nd May	30th May	5th June	13th June
21st June	28th June	5th July	13th July
20th July	27th July	3rd August	11th August
19th August	25th August	2nd September	10th September
17th September	24th September	1st October	10th October
28th September	5th October	13th October	21st October
16th October	23rd October	31st October	8th November
15th November	22nd November	30th November	8th December
14th December	21st December	30th December	

THE NATURAL GARDENER

2021 MOON CALENDAR

New Moon	First Quarter	Full Moon	Last Quarter
			6th January
13th January	20th January	28th January	4th February
11th February	19th February	27th February	6th March
13th March	21st March	28th March	4th April
12th April	20th April	27th April	3rd May
11th May	19th May	26th May	2nd June
10th June	18th June	24th June	1st July
10th July	17th July	24th July	31st July
8th August	15th August	22nd August	30th August
7th September	13th September	21st September	29th September
6th October	13th October	20th October	28th October
4th November	11th November	19th November	27th November
4th December	11th December	19th December	27th December

MY 2020–2022 MOON GARDENING CALENDARS

2022 MOON CALENDAR

New Moon	First Quarter	Full Moon	Last Quarter
2nd January	9th January	17th January	25th January
1st February	8th February	16th February	23rd February
2nd March	10th March	18th March	25th March
1st April	9th April	16th April	23rd April
30th April	9th May	16th May	22nd May
30th May	7th June	14th June	21st June
29th June	7th July	13th July	20th July
28th July	5th August	12th August	19th August
27th August	3rd September	10th September	17th September
25th September	3rd October	9th October	17th October
25th October	1st November	8th November	16th November
23rd November	30th November	8th December	16th December
23rd December	30th December		

235

Acknowledgements

I would like to say a big thank you to my good friend Jim Rickards for the many hours of work, under daylight and moonlight, writing and editing all the material in this book. Without him I do not think I would have been able to compile it. Knowing the subject is one thing, putting it on paper is another.

Great thanks to our editor, Toby Buchan, for his long hours on the project and unfailing support. And, of course, to John Blake for contacting me after reading an article about my lunacy and persuading me it wasn't such a bad idea to put it out there for others to judge.

Last but not least, thanks to my wife Olive who has helped patiently with my research, organised me without grumbles, and pastied my frustrations away.